Published by Avenue Media Solutions

www.avenuemediasolutions.com

© Neil Thompson 2019 All Rights Reserved

Lessons for Living

101 Top Tips for Optimal Well-being at Work and Beyond

By

Neil Thompson

Keep making a difference!
Best wishes,
Neil

Contents

About the author — p. 5
About Avenue Media Solutions — p. 6
Preface — p. 7
Introduction — p. 8

Part One: Making Sense of Happiness and Well-being — p. 10

What is well-being? — p. 11
What is happiness? — p. 17
Why all the fuss about well-being and happiness? — p. 18
What can we do to promote well-being? — p. 20
Protecting the environment — p. 23
Realism — p. 23
Conclusion — p. 24

Part Two: 101 Top Tips for Optimal Well-being — p. 25

Introduction to Part Two — p. 26
1. Effective communication: topic and comment — p. 28
2. Head and heart work at different speeds — p. 29
3. Who is being awkward? — p. 30
4. Silence does not equal consent — p. 31
5. Tolerate silence — p. 32
6. You don't know how I feel — p. 33
7. Dadirri listening — p. 34
8. There's no need to shout — p. 35
9. Customer care: getting it right — p. 36
10. Find the right pace — p. 37
11. Conflict can be constructive — p. 38

12. Accept what you can't change — p. 39
13. Everyone has 24 hours in their day — p. 40
14. Don't let forms shape your practice — p. 41
15. Question routines — p. 42
16. Make a note of important ideas — p. 43
17. Start your own book of the month club — p. 44
18. Why here? Why now? — p. 45
19. Don't reply in anger — p. 46
20. Say thank you — p. 47
21. Choose the right communication method — p. 48
22. Clarify boundaries — p. 49
23. Live to fight another day — p. 50
24. I-Thou, not I-it — p. 51
25. Look for reasons, not causes — p. 52
26. Dress for the part — p. 53
27. Use 'holding' emails — p. 54
28. Don't try to do the impossible — p. 55
29. Take a break — p. 56
30. Use of self — p. 57
31. Try Garfinkeling — p. 58
32. Acknowledge problems, but focus on solutions — p. 59
33. Respect cultural differences — p. 60
34. Aim for adult-adult — p. 61
35. Don't take it personally — p. 62
36. Remove distractions where possible — p. 63
37. Use distractions where possible — p. 64
38. Recognize warning signs of aggression and potential violence — p. 65
39. Use reframing — p. 66
40. Avoid rumination — p. 67
41. Failure is part of success — p. 68
42. Don't be a rescuer — p. 69
43. Don't speak (or write) officialese — p. 70

44. Set out your stall	p. 71
45. Keep your records up to date	p. 72
46. Need to know, not nice to know	p. 73
47. Fail to plan and you plan to fail	p. 74
48. Apologize where necessary	p. 75
49. Save face	p. 76
50. Tune into grief	p. 77
51. Be prepared for meetings	p. 78
52. Manage your own learning	p. 79
53. Compartmentalize home and work	p. 80
54. Use touch appropriately	p. 81
55. Why helps with how	p. 82
56. Be open to learning from mistakes	p. 83
57. Make the best use of your best time	p. 84
58. Allow time for recovery	p. 85
59. There's no point rushing	p. 86
60. Negotiate your workload	p. 87
61. Recognize boundaries of responsibility	p. 88
62. Get the information you need	p. 89
63. Don't allow other people's pressures to distort your priorities	p. 90
64. Assess, don't assume	p. 91
65. Remember that values are not set in stone	p. 92
66. Don't get too comfortable	p. 93
67. Put yourself in their shoes	p. 94
68. Don't assume you can't make a difference	p. 95
69. Don't underestimate the importance of feedback	p. 96
70. Make use of perspective	p. 97
71. Focus on what motivates	p. 98
72. Define the problem	p. 99
73. Be prepared for conflict	p. 100
74. Complain to the right person	p. 101
75. Hear the silence	p. 102

76. Projects are gardens not buildings	p. 103
77. Don't assume you are wrong	p. 104
78. Accept what you can't change	p. 105
79. Cultivate self-awareness	p. 106
80. Don't reinvent the wheel	p. 107
81. Practise self-leadership	p. 108
82. More is not necessarily better	p. 109
83. Challenge elegantly	p. 110
84. Make it happen – carpe diem	p. 111
85. Direct concerns to where the power is	p. 112
86. Develop an internal locus of control	p. 113
87. Begin with the end in mind	p. 114
88. Capitalize on crisis	p. 115
89. Beware of cloning	p. 116
90. Step back from time to time	p. 117
91. Choose your time and place	p. 118
92. Believe in yourself	p. 119
93. Give yourself thinking time	p. 120
94. Invest time to save time	p. 121
95. Think before you write	p. 122
96. Don't rely on common sense	p. 123
97. Don't drop hints	p. 124
98. Take account of trauma	p. 125
99. Smile!	p. 126
100. Value your time	p. 127
101. Recognize that bullying is not strong leadership	p. 128
Conclusion	p. 129
References	p. 130
Other learning resources by Neil Thompson	p. 133
Connect with Neil online	p. 135
Other Avenue Media Solutions learning resources	p. 136

About the author

Very many people have come to rely on Dr Neil Thompson as a guide and mentor, not only on their learning journey, but also on their whole outlook on life, people, problems and potential. With an impeccable academic pedigree, an outstanding publications record and a wealth of direct experience of making a positive difference in a number of ways, he stands out as an invaluable source of wisdom and guidance.

His work is based on the central idea that:

**Where there are PEOPLE, there will be PROBLEMS,
but there will also be POTENTIAL**

Neil's career has revolved around helping people tackle those problems and realize that potential. This has given him the well-deserved reputation for being a powerful source of motivation and morale and an inspiring guide on what he likes to call the journey from surviving to thriving.

His website and blog are at www.NeilThompson.info and you can get a free subscription to his e-newsletter at: http://www.humsndolutions.org.uk.

About Avenue Media Solutions

Avenue Media Solutions offers a range of learning resources:

- Books and practice manuals
- Training manuals
- E-books
- E-courses
- The Avenue Professional Development Programme
- DVDs

We are also able to draw on our expertise in communication to offer:

- Low-cost video production
- Social media marketing strategy development

The two linking threads across our work are **people** and **communication**. Throughout our work we recognize the significance of the human element of people's working lives and the central role of communication. So, whether, it is a matter of personal and professional development or getting your important marketing message across, our focus is on helping you achieve the best results at value-for-money prices.

www.avenuemediasolutions.com

Preface

In a career spanning five decades I have been privileged to work with a wide variety of people to help them fulfil their potential. My work has revolved around what I like to call the three Ps: People, Problems, Potential – or, to explain it more fully: where there are people, there will be problems, but there will also be potential. So, my role in various contexts and settings has been to help people tackle their problems and fulfil their potential.

This book is a contribution to my efforts to be as helpful as I can. It distils considerable wisdom drawn from my extensive experience and study, and from the learning I have gained from working alongside some very talented and inspiring people.

The book is in two parts. The first is an extended essay on the subject of well-being, what it is, how it relates to happiness and how we can take steps to maximize it. In a sense, it lays down a foundation of learning to serve as a basis of understanding to underpin Part Two. It is therefore presented as food for thought to get you considering the issues involved.

Part Two is a set of 101 practical tips that are intended to help you benefit from the learning I have done over all these years, both directly from my own experience and indirectly from the experience of having worked in various educational roles that have given me insights into what has worked well for other people. Each tip is laid out with space for your own notes. This is because it is important that you 'tailor' the tips to suit your own circumstances, goals, aspirations, needs and challenges. They are not there to be followed blindly and uncritically, but used more as food for thought to get you reflecting on the key issues involved.

Introduction

Well-being is not a new idea, but it has certainly been attracting far more attention these days than was previously the case. I speculate below as to why that has come to be the case, but for now we should just recognize that well-being is increasingly being seen as an important topic. Happiness is also not a new term, but again is attracting a great deal of attention (see for example, Layard, 2006, Ricard, 2006). Some people use the terms well-being and happiness more or less interchangeably, but in reality, they are quite different, albeit linked to one another in some ways.

So, we have two important concepts that are generating a lot of interest, but unfortunately both of them are characterized by a degree of oversimplification. This book is intended to clear up some of the confusion and present a clear and accessible overview of the issues involved, but without oversimplifying them – that is, it has been written in such a way as to do justice to the complexities involved.

One important underpinning for the book and the knowledge base on which it is based is the key notion of *critically reflective practice*. By reflective practice I mean an approach that involves thinking carefully about the issues we are dealing with, drawing on our knowledge, skills and values, as opposed to just reacting in a habitual or unthinking way. By *critically* reflective practice, I mean practice that questions taken-for-granted assumptions and looks beneath the surface (rather than just taking everything at face value) and looks at the broader picture and the social context involved (rather than focusing narrowly on the individual). To develop a fuller understanding of critically reflective practice, see Thompson and Thompson (2018).

The book is divided into two parts. Part One is, in turn, divided into four main sections. In the first section we explore what is meant by well-being and look at different types of well-being and how they relate to one another. From this we will see that well-being is a more complex subject than people generally realize. In the second section I discuss the notion of happiness and try to show that there is more to this too than meets the eye. In the third section I try to explain why well-being and happiness seem to be such popular topics these days. In the final section I look at various ways in which we can promote well-being and happiness. There are no magic answers or secret formulas, but there are steps we can take – individually and collectively – to promote well-being and happiness.

Part Two comprises a series of short tips distilled from my 40+ years of working in a professional capacity to help people address the problems they face and to realize their potential as fully as possible. Some of the tips overlap to a certain extent, in the sense that they occupy similar territory, but this helps to highlight the interconnectedness of so much of human behavior.

I very much hope that you will find the book of interest and benefit and that the thinking and understanding it stimulates will prove to be empowering.

Part One

Making Sense of Well-being

What is well-being?

In my view, to understand what well-being is, it is helpful first to look at what it is not – that is, to clear up some misunderstandings. First it is often used alongside health, and we could be forgiven, then for seeing it as an aspect of health. Indeed, many people use health and well-being more or less interchangeably. For example, many discussions of 'health and well-being' – whether in print, online or in speech – are mainly, if not exclusively, about health, with the well-being element somehow falling off the edge. This is particularly the case in relation to workplace well-being (a topic I shall return to below), where so often the discussions are actually about health in the workplace.

However, this way of using the term 'well-being' is misleading and unhelpful. This is because, while health and well-being are interconnected in some ways, they are certainly not the same thing. This is confirmed by the fact that it is possible to have health without well-being and vice versa. Consider the following examples:

➢ A person may be in excellent health but have a very low level of well-being, perhaps because they are grieving, are having relationship difficulties, are being bullied or any other problem that may not directly affect health, but which will almost certainly undermine any sense of well-being.

➢ A person may be in very poor health, but none the less have a very strong foundation of well-being. Some people manage to have excellent quality of life despite poor health. Perhaps an extreme – but none the less not uncommon example – would be someone who is terminally ill, but is determined to make the most of what is left of their life (see the discussion of spirituality below).

Clearly, then, health and well-being can and do influence each other much of the time, but it is still important to be able to distinguish between the two if we are to avoid confusion and oversimplification.

What also complicates matters is that many people use the term 'wellness' as a synonym for well-being, while it would be wiser to associate that term with health than with well-being. For example, MacDonald (2005) writes about wellness at work and, at times, it is not clear whether she is referring specifically to health matters or more broadly to well-being concerns.

It is also important to distinguish between welfare and well-being. Again, there is some degree of overlap between the two terms, but it can be problematic not to distinguish between the two. This is because welfare can often have a degree of stigma associated with it, whereas well-being does not. Welfare implies concern for others. While well-being *can* involve concern for others (see the discussion of social well-being below), it does not necessarily involve this.

So, if well-being is not health and it is not welfare, what is it? At its simplest, well-being is a matter of quality of life. For the more complex answer we need to understand the different types or dimensions of well-being. One way of understanding this is captured in the idea of 'Getting WISE about well-being', with WISE spelling out: **w**orkplace well-being; **i**ndividual well-being; **s**ocial well-being; and **e**nvironmental well-being. We should also not lose sight of children's well-being. As a starting point, then, let us now consider each of these five aspects of well-being:

Workplace well-being

For many years there was a school of thought that emphasized the importance of 'staff care' – that is, the idea that, if organizations want to get the best out of their staff, they need to look after them, to make sure that their needs are met and that they are not being mistreated in any way (for example, through bullying or having to wrestle with excessive workloads). In recent years, there has been an increasing emphasis on such matters and the term 'staff care' has now been largely replaced by that of 'workplace well-being' (or sometimes, 'employee well-being').

A commitment to workplace well-being involves the following key features:

➤ Making sure that staff (and managers) feel valued and supported, with the benefits of effective leadership.

➤ Protecting all employees from 'toxic' experiences (stress; bullying and harassment; aggression and violence; and so on).

➤ Recognizing that, where there are people, there will be problems, and being prepared to address these problems constructively and supportively, rather than simply brushing them under the carpet. Such problems include: conflicts; drug and alcohol problems; loss, grief and trauma; mental health problems and so on. If such problems are not recognized and dealt with, the result is likely to be higher levels of sickness absence, recruitment and retention problems and a reduction in the quality and quantity of work.

Given the importance of work in the lives of so many people, we can see that workplace well-being is a very significant set of considerations and one worthy of careful attention.

Individual well-being

There are various aspects of individual well-being but the two I am going to focus on here in particular are health and spirituality:

➤ *Health* Health, of course, is not simply a matter of absence of disease. It can be understood more broadly to incorporate exercise, diet, sleep and other lifestyle factors that affect our quality of life and can be significant when it comes to preventing health problems in the future. While it is a mistake to equate health with well-being, it would also be a mistake not to recognize that health is an important factor in relation to quality of life and therefore well-being.

> *Spirituality* For many people their spirituality comes from a particular religion or faith community. However, everyone, whether religious or not, has spiritual needs – the need for meaning and a sense of purpose and direction, for hope and 'connectedness' to other people and, overall, a sense of who we are and how we fit into the wider world. There are various factors (grief, for example) that can lead to difficulties in achieving a sense of spiritual well-being.

Of course, these two sets of factors influence one another, and each can help or hinder the other. From the point of view of promoting well-being, then, these are both topics that are worthy of close attention.

Social well-being

There are various factors that have a bearing on wider society – for example, such issues as social justice, social inclusion and related matters. Basically, social well-being is concerned with trying to ensure that the way society works is based on such key values as fairness, democracy, citizen participation, equality, valuing diversity and inclusiveness. There is therefore a strong political element to social well-being.

A commitment to social well-being involves:

> *Tackling discrimination and oppression* Promoting equality and social justice involves tackling discrimination and oppression wherever we encounter them. This is a complex and demanding undertaking but an essential foundation for social well-being (Thompson, 2018).

> *Addressing social problems* Poverty, crime, homelessness and abuse of various kinds are just some of the problems we face. If these are left unchecked, then not only will those people directly subject to these problems experience great suffering, but society as a whole will be impoverished (Thompson, 2017).

> *Promoting citizenship, participation and democracy* Getting more people more fully involved in how our societies are governed can be seen to be a positive step towards greater social well-being, as it helps to move us away from the twin evils of elitism and bureaucracy.

It is unrealistic to expect that we can bring about major changes in the short term in the problems and destructive processes that stand in the way of greater social well-being, but there are important steps that we can take to make improvements in the short term and contribute to a longer-term goal of creating a better society.

Environmental well-being

Concern about the damage we are doing to our planet home has been growing steadily for some years now, as more and more people become environmentally conscious. However, whether that concern is growing fast enough and whether the changes we are making as a result of that awareness are sufficient remain difficult and worrying questions.

A commitment to environmental well-being involves:

> Being aware of the various ways in which we are harming the planet (our environmental 'footprint').

> Being aware of the steps we need to take to change the situation for the positive and making sure we take those steps wherever possible.

> 'Spreading the word' – making other people aware of the problems and threats and the potential solutions.

Going 'green' has become something of a fashion for many people, but we need to make sure that what we are doing in ecological terms is more than following a fad. Focusing on environmental well-being can help us to put environmental matters more firmly on the agenda.

Children's well-being

There are no guaranteed, foolproof ways of making sure that children and young people are protected from abuse and harm or that their rights are safeguarded. However, there are important things we can do to put children's well-being more firmly on the agenda. These include:

➢ Doing everything we reasonably can – individually and collectively – to protect children and young people from abuse and neglect.

➢ Promote children's rights where possible (this does not mean giving children licence to do whatever they want, but it does mean that being young should not deny anyone their rights).

➢ Involve children and young people in decision-making processes (especially about their own well-being), to make sure their voices are heard and that they have the opportunity to learn about responsibility.

I would argue that these issues are (or should be) matters of concern for everyone, not just for parents and for professionals working with children and young people. Of course, it goes without saying that how we treat the children and young people of today will make a significant difference to how people are treated in the future by the next generation of decision makers.

***

I have provided an overview of these five areas of well-being separately, one after the other. The reality, of course, is more complex than this. A more accurate picture of well-being is one in which these different aspects will interact and influence one another (for example, workplace well-being will have an impact on individual well-being and vice versa). In order to promote well-being, then, we need a fairly broad understanding of the topic to ensure that we can see how the different parts interrelate.

Indeed, this was one of the main reasons for the development of the *humansolutions* website: to provide a holistic picture of well-being that emphasizes the need to appreciate how the different elements are interconnected (www.humansolutions.org.uk). This should have the effect of: (i) preventing 'silo' thinking (that is, people with interests in one particular area of well-being focusing narrowly on their own issues and failing to see them as part of the bigger picture); and (ii) providing a platform for strategic alliances – that is, not only for people with specific interests in one field to support one another and learn from each other, but also for these positive processes to occur *across* areas of interest, thereby enabling a wide range of people who have the shared goal of promoting well-being in all its forms to support each other and learn from one another.

What is happiness?

Happiness, like well-being, is closely related to the idea of quality of life, but the key difference is that well-being is something that endures (or can endure) over time, while happiness can more usefully be seen as 'episodic' – that is, we feel happy for a while for a particular reason, but this feeling will fade over time as we return to our normal state – until the next 'episode' when something else raises our spirits above their normal level (or 'homeostasis', to use the technical term). It can be helpful to think of happiness in terms of joy and well-being in terms of contentment.

Although some authors use the term 'happiness' to refer to an enduring sense of 'positive affect' (that is, feeling good) – see, for example, Ricard (2015) – this raises the question of how realistic it is to be happy all the time. Indeed, if we were joyful all the time, would the concept of joy continue to have any meaning?

Happiness and well-being are closely linked, in so far as the higher our level of well-being, the more often we will have episodes of happiness – and, the more episodes of happiness we have, the higher our level of well-being is likely to be.

While it clearly makes sense to 'seek happiness', it is both naive and unrealistic to expect to be able to achieve a state of constant happiness. Well-being is certainly a more realistic goal to aim for, and from that we have opportunities for episodes of happiness, moments of joy.

Why all the fuss about well-being and happiness?

The terms 'well-being' and 'happiness' have become hot topics in recent years. As with social phenomena generally, there is no single, definitive cause, but rather a set of factors that combine to produce the changes.

These factors can be seen to include:

> ➢ *Changes in the public sector* Managerialism is an approach to public service that has emerged over the last two decades, fuelled by the growing strength of 'neoliberalism' as a political ideology (Thompson, 2017). The net result has been a shift away from public service professionals being trusted to produce optimal results based on a degree of autonomy towards a more bureaucratic, top-down approach focusing on 'performance indicators' which, sadly, can be seen to have had a profoundly demoralizing effect and contributed to an epidemic of stress and workplace dissatisfaction (Thompson, 2019). Clearly this has major implications not only for workplace well-being, but also for the individual well-being of those directly affected (managers, staff and clients) and social well-being more broadly in view of the fact that the erosion of a commitment to public service can be seen to be detrimental to society as a whole. In addition, these changes in the public sector have had a knock-on effect for the third sector and thus for voluntary and community organisations.

- *Changes in the private sector* The development of 'business process re-engineering' (BPR) as an approach to management and business can be seen to have had a similar effect in the world of business. Although not a new idea (see Micklethwait and Wooldridge, 1996), its effects have been cumulative over a number of years. The basic idea behind the approach is that businesses can optimize their profits if they slim down processes to the minimum required. This includes slimming down staffing levels to their minimum which (i) has produced a high number of layoffs (euphemistically referred to as 'downsizing' or even 'rightsizing'); and (ii) often placed inordinate pressure on those staff who remain (for example, through there being no spare staffing capacity to cover illness, exceptional levels of demand or other unplanned-for contingencies). This approach can be seen to be a major contributor to a wide range of workplace problems (stress, bullying, conflict, mental health problems and so on) and therefore both a significant obstacle to well-being and a significant contributor to why well-being has been receiving so much attention.

- *Changes in the world economy* James (2007) writes about 'affluenza', a malaise he associates with unfettered capitalism (what, in a later work – James, 2008 – he refers to as 'selfish capitalism'). These publications were written before the recession precipitated by high-risk mortgage lending to 'sub-prime' markets – that is, by practices in the financial sector that prioritized the chance of higher profits over the danger of a collapse of the economy, with all the misery, suffering and threats to well-being that this brought. The financial pressures of recession and economic austerity can have the effect of leading people to reconsider what they value, to review what is important to them and thus what their sources of well-being are.

- *The emerging popularity of 'positive psychology'* Positive psychology emphasizes the idea that optimism is an essential basis for happiness. It has become a very fashionable and influential approach and is now supported by an extensive literature base – for example, Seligman (2006), Boniwell and Tunariu (2019). I shall return to this topic below.

> *The growing interest in spirituality* Traditionally spirituality is associated with religion, although it is now increasingly being recognized that religion is just one way of expressing our spirituality (Moss, 2005). There is now also growing awareness of the links between spirituality and social and personal problems. For example, Coyte *et al.* (2007) is a collection of readings which explores the significance of spirituality in relation to mental health.

The fact that well-being is such a 'hot' topic is a mixed blessing. On the positive side, the increased attention gives us the opportunity to develop our understanding of well-being and related matters and to explore ways of using that knowledge to improve quality of life and address the problems and obstacles that block or undermine it. However, on the debit side, with popularity comes oversimplification, which in turn paves the way for a range of people who jump on a bandwagon in promoting their own version of some sort of magic solution.

What can we do to promote well-being and happiness?

With a subject matter as complex as this it would be highly inappropriate to try to come up with some sort of simple and definitive answer to how well-being and happiness can be increased. However, it would also be a mistake to assume that there is nothing that can be done. The wisest, most constructive way forward lies somewhere in between those two extremes. I shall therefore offer some suggestions as to what steps can be taken in the desired direction, while acknowledging that this is far from an exhaustive or comprehensive list of potential measures that could be adopted.

Layard (2006) discusses seven factors that contribute to what he refers to as happiness, what I would describe as well-being (that is not just a temporary state of 'feeling good'). He refers to these as 'The Big Seven':

> *Family relationships* Positive family relationships can add significantly to well-being, but it also has to be recognized that problems in families (child abuse, domestic violence) can be extremely detrimental. Efforts dedicated to promoting positive family relationships and to address family problems (through social work, for example) can therefore be recognized as important contributions to well-being.

> *Financial situation* It is perhaps not surprising that financial matters are so significant, given that money can offer access to so many other goods and opportunities (although we should also note that an obsession with material wealth can be seen to undermine well-being – Boldt, 1999). The work of Wilson and Pickett (2010, 2018) have shown that a reduction in inequality would be of benefit to everyone and not just to those at the lower end of the income scale. A stronger focus on equality can therefore be identified as a significant contribution to enhanced levels of well-being.

> *Work* Simply being in work can prove to be of considerable help, as the disbenefits of unemployment show. Layard comments that unemployment:

> > reduces income but it also reduces happiness directly by reducing self-respect and social relationships created by work. When people become unemployed, their happiness falls much less because of the loss of income than because of the loss of work itself.
> > (2006, p. 67)

The significance of work as a 'happiness factor' highlights the significance of workplace well-being, in so far as the workplace can also be a site of major problems (stress, bullying, violence and so on – Thompson and Bates, 2009). Measures to address unemployment can therefore be a significant strand of concerted efforts to enhance well-being, as can a commitment to taking workplace well-being seriously.

- *Community and friends* Our relationships with other people can, of course, be highly problematic at times (reflecting Sartre's famous claim that 'hell is other people' – Sartre, 2000), but they can also be a great source of happiness. Investing in community development and greater opportunities for people to develop social capital therefore has much to commend it. Jordan (2007) discusses the idea of 'an interpersonal economy' as opposed to the conventional notion of the financial economy. Too strong an emphasis on the latter (and the materialism on which it is based) undermines well-being, while greater connection with other people (social capital) enhances it.

- *Health* The relationship between health and happiness is a complex one, but it is clear that health issues do have a bearing on happiness (and, indeed, well-being). While improved health will not necessarily increase well-being in all cases, better health is clearly a worthwhile goal to pursue.

- *Personal freedom* This introduces a broader, sociopolitical dimension, as Layard contends that the political regime in which people live – and the degree of liberty it extends to its citizens or subjects – will have a significant bearing on their happiness. The defence of civil liberties is therefore an important basis for promoting well-being.

- *Personal values* Values are those things that are important to us, the principles and beliefs that guide our thoughts, feelings and actions (Thompson and Moss, 2019). They are part and parcel of our spirituality, and so this aspect of Layard's framework chimes well with our earlier discussion of spiritual well-being. People can easily become so absorbed in their work and/or home pressures that they lose sight of their values. Revisiting our values can therefore be a valuable step in promoting spiritual well-being.

While these are important ways in which we can invest in enhanced levels of well-being, I would want them to be supplemented by (at least) two further considerations, environmental well-being and the importance of 'realism'.

Protecting the environment

Earlier I emphasized the importance of environmental well-being. Given the significance of this I would argue that all our well-being-oriented activities need to be underpinned by efforts to address the major environmental challenges we face. It is disappointing that so much of the literature relating to well-being has little or nothing to say about the harm we are doing to the planet.

A commitment to environmental well-being can also bring other benefits in terms of – for example – spiritual well-being (being part of something bigger than ourselves, feeling part of a meaningful enterprise that gives us a sense of direction) and/or social well-being (bringing people together in empowering ways). We should therefore be careful not to neglect the environmental dimension.

Realism

I referred earlier to the emphasis in positive psychology on optimism, of always expecting the best. In an earlier work (Thompson, 2015) I have criticized that approach for being unbalanced, for not adequately recognizing that a more pessimistic outlook can at times be a more appropriate response to our circumstances (Dienstag, 2006). In place of a one-sided focus on optimism, I proposed an approach characterized by realism – that is, by a recognition that the glass is both half empty *and* half full.

Seeing only the positives or only the negatives is, in my view, a highly dangerous distortion of reality. Being tuned in to the fact that life is characterized by both great beauty and joy and immense pain and suffering (realism) provides a stronger platform for coping with life's challenges than a simplistic choice between focusing only (or primarily) on either the positives (optimism) or the negatives (pessimism). For a powerful critique of positive psychology see Hedges (2009).

Conclusion to Part One

It is clear that well-being and the related concept of happiness are significant areas of interest at the current time. While I welcome this interest in such important topics as these, I have significant concerns about how both these concepts (and the relationship between them) are prone to oversimplification. This is partly a process of 'commodification', with so many people seeking to make money from offering 'solutions' to the various problems associated with well-being and happiness. Some of these products and services are rooted in what is basically a sound understanding but which has become oversimplified, while others are simply a modern form of 'snake oil' being peddled to cure all our well-being ills.

While there is little point pursuing simplistic magic solutions, there is much that can be achieved from concerted efforts (individual and collective) to make well-being more than a fashionable discussion point and build on the important foundations we have for improving quality of life in so many different ways.

Part Two

101 Top Tips for Optimal Well-being

Introduction

My 40+ year career has involved a number of jobs in different sectors, but, as noted earlier, a recurring theme throughout has been *people*. Whatever work I have undertaken, success has, to a large degree, depended on being able to work effectively with people. Long ago I came to the conclusion that, where there are people, there will be problems – but there will also be potential. More or less all of my work has revolved around that core idea.

The reason I say 'where there are people, there will be problems', is that everyone has their own perspective on life, on what is important, on how things are and how things should be. So, it is not surprising that there will be conflicts and difficulties arising before too long once people come together. But, with the right skill and the right attitude, these problems can be managed very effectively most of the time.

But it isn't just a matter of addressing the problems that arise, it's also about recognizing – and capitalizing on – the huge positive potential when people come together. Managing 'people problems' and realizing the potential that people have, individually and collectively, is skilled work, and much of my published work has focused precisely on these issues (see the details below). Part Two builds on my earlier work. It provides 101 'top tips' – that is, pieces of practical information, drawn from my extensive experience of working with people and their problems, to serve as food for thought and give you a basis to work from.

'Food for thought' is an important phrase. These tips are not intended to be used mindlessly or mechanistically. My hope is that, for each one, you will give the issues some thought and develop the ideas concerned to suit your own circumstances and your own existing knowledge and skills.

Unfortunately, there is a large 'self-help' industry that offers all sorts of solutions to the challenges we face and, while much of it is of value, a great deal of it is very simplistic 'guru speak' that is the modern version of snake oil geared towards gullible people naively looking for a magic answer to their problems (see Briers, 2012, for a critique of what he calls 'psychobabble'). There are no magic answers, of course, but there are lessons we can learn from other people's experiences of tackling various life challenges – hence the title of *Lessons for Living*. The tips presented here in Part Two should therefore be understood in this context and not as simplistic answers.

Space has deliberately been left on each page for you to make your own notes and thereby record your own reflections.

1. Effective communication: topic and comment

Communication goes awry quite regularly, which is not surprising when you think about how much of it we do in any given day. One common way in which communication breaks down is when what is said (or written) does not cover both topic and comment. The topic is what we are talking about and the comment is what we are saying about it. They can be articulated separately ('You know that book on stress I lent you? [topic] I will need it back if that's OK [comment]') or together ('Can you please let me have back that book on stress I lent you?'). Either is fine when both topic and comment are covered, but often, there is a topic identified, but it is not clear what the comment is ('You've got my book on stress, haven't you?'). Is this simply a comment to check that the book is still in their possession or is it an indirect request for it to be returned? It is not clear. Similarly, effective communication can be undermined by making a comment without specifying the topic – something that commonly evokes a response along the lines of: 'Sorry, I'm not clear what you're referring to?' or 'Sorry, I'm not with you'. What can be much worse, though, is when the topic is not specified and the person listening makes a false assumption about what the topic is – and then we have a recipe for major misunderstanding and miscommunication. So, it pays to make sure that we are always clear in communicating both topic and comment.

2. Head and heart work at different speeds

From time to time we find ourselves in situations where we are finding it difficult to comprehend what has happened – times of loss, crisis or sudden change, for example. It is as if our head knows, but our heart hasn't caught up, and so 'it doesn't seem real' can be a thought that runs through our mind. This is a perfectly normal phenomenon and nothing to be concerned about in itself. However, we need to be wary of two potential problems. One is that, when we find ourselves in such a situation, we may make decisions that we later regret because we have been destabilized by the change that has occurred. For example, some people can respond quite rashly in situations where they are confused about what is happening. Second, if we are trying to help somebody who is in a 'heart hasn't caught up with head' situation, we have to bear in mind that they may not be taking on board what we are saying to them because of the sense of emotional shock they are experiencing. We therefore have to choose our moments carefully in interacting with someone in such circumstances.

3. Who is being awkward?

It is not uncommon for us to find ourselves in situations where we are wondering: 'Why is so and so being so awkward?'. In such circumstances we tend to focus on their behaviour or attitude, but this can be misleading. That is because the chances are that, while we are thinking *they* are being awkward, they are probably thinking *we* are being awkward. So, what can often happen is that a situation that is rooted in a conflict between two parties is not recognized as such by either of them, each putting the difficulties down to the other's 'awkward' behaviour. While some people are often uncooperative for their own reasons, in the majority of cases believing that someone is being awkward should alert us to a conflict situation which should be addressed as such – that is, we need to look at the situation in terms of the interactions between us (and any conflicts of interest, perspective, goals or values that might be underpinning them) and not simply in terms of the other person's behaviour.

4. Silence does not equal consent

This is a mistake I made many times early in my career: making a suggestion or proposal, having no one object to it and then assuming that the lack of explicit objection constituted agreement to what I had put forward. I then had the unpleasant experience of watching my plans fall apart as people did not cooperate with them or play their part in moving things forward – or even, on some occasions, actively sabotaged what I was trying to do. It only slowly became apparent to me that they were never really 'on board' in terms of what I had proposed but, for whatever reason, had chosen not to voice their disagreement. So, there is a very important lesson in this: we cannot assume that silence equals consent. A lack of explicit disagreement is not the same as agreement. So, if we are relying on others to bring our plans to fruition, we need to make the effort to ensure that they are genuinely in agreement and make it clear that if they are not, they should say so.

5. Tolerate silence

In working with people, emotions are never very far away. Being able to tune in to other people's emotions, to be aware of our own and get the balance of head and heart right is often referred to as 'emotional intelligence'. A key part of this is being able to tolerate silences. When someone is distressed or otherwise in the grip of strong emotions, they may fall silent, and that silence can feel very uncomfortable for us. We can be very tempted to jump in and ask a question or just fill the gap in some way. Understandable though this may be, it can be quite problematic because we are, in effect, giving the person concerned the message that dealing with our own discomfort is more important than giving them the emotional space they need. If we are able to resist the temptation of filling the silence, we give the much more positive and supportive message that we are there for them, that they are not facing their difficulties unsupported. And what an important message that can be.

6. You don't know how I feel

Many people confuse *sympathy* (sharing the same feelings as someone else) and *empathy* (being able to recognize someone else's feelings and being able to respond appropriately, but without necessarily having those feelings ourselves), while others settle for *apathy*, in a state of semi-burnout. But clearly empathy is what we need to aim for: being able to be supportive of others who are wrestling with emotional issues, but without facing the same emotional challenges ourselves. However, what is very clear is that this is not simply a matter of saying: 'I know how you feel'. This is a very unhelpful and potentially quite counterproductive way to respond, partly because: (i) we do not know how someone else feels (for example, if I am helping someone who has just lost their father, the fact that I have lost my father does not mean that I know how they feel, as our respective experiences of losing a father may have evoked very different feelings); and (ii) making such a comment means we are focusing on our own feelings, rather than those of the person we are trying to help.

7. Dadirri listening

Listening, of course, is more than just hearing. It is about paying attention to someone in a way that creates a genuine human connection. Sometimes that connection is enough to enable the person concerned to feel stronger, more confident and better supported in dealing with their difficulties. Listening is an important first step in terms of exploring potential solutions, but at times listening is enough on its own to find the strength to move forward positively. 'Dadirri' is a concept drawn from Australian aboriginal culture which refers to the type of listening that creates that all-important bond, listening that gives a strong and genuine message that we are concerned and that we are here to help without judgement. It could be described as listening with our heart, rather than just with our ears. When you have been on the receiving end of such listening you will know about it, as you will feel the positive, empowering effects of it. Learning how to develop dadirri listening is therefore an important step forward for us to take.

8. There's no need to shout

Stereotyping can be seen as a very real danger when you consider how often we are fed inaccurate, distorted and oversimplified stereotypes by the media. There is therefore a very strong need to be 'stereotype aware' and try to makes sure as far as possible that we do not allow ourselves to be influenced by them. One such stereotype that I have come across time and time again is the assumption that certain people are likely to be hard of hearing and that it is therefore necessary to shout. Older people are a prime target for this type of stereotyping, but disabled people are not immune to it either. While the incidence of hearing loss is indeed greater in the older population than in the general population, this is far removed from assuming that all older (or disabled) people have a degree of hearing loss. It is easy enough to adjust our volume if we need to, and so there is no need to shout as a general rule, as that just reinforces stereotypes and can be intimidating. But, such is the prevalence of stereotypical thinking that very many people resort to raising their voice without even realizing that they are doing so.

9. Customer care: getting it right

We don't get a second chance when it comes to first impressions, and yet sadly many organizations pay relatively little attention to how people are greeted when they have their first contact with the organization concerned. If we want to make a positive difference, then it is important that we get off to a good start by giving a positive, welcoming message, letting people know that they are valued and respected. Much of 'customer care' is basic communication skills, but there can sometimes be additional challenges involved (for example, where someone is irate or threatening). Of course, however difficult such situations may be, we need to remain focused and respectful – even if we feel very uncomfortable. This will help to make sure that, after the person concerned has calmed down, they will appreciate how well they were treated. If, on the contrary, we allow the tensions involved to prevent us from being helpful and supportive, we can be creating significant difficulties for ourselves (and/or our colleagues) further down the road if the message we are giving out is that resolving our own discomfort is more important than providing genuine customer care.

10. Find the right pace

When it comes to working with people and their problems getting the pace right is perhaps one of the most difficult things to do, but do it we must. That is because if we are going too slowly we may miss opportunities to move forward – for example, 'missing the boat' when someone is in crisis and motivated to make important changes. If we move too swiftly, we may create (or exacerbate) insecurity and anxiety and thereby hamper progress in terms of whatever need we are trying to meet or problem we are trying to solve. So, how do we judge what is the best pace? There is no hard and fast rule, but mainly it comes from looking closely at the situation, gauging reactions to our input and picking up the clues about how comfortable or otherwise the person(s) involved appear to be. Difficult though this may be, it gets easier with experience, provided that we stay tuned in to the need to consider pace as an important feature of our efforts to help.

11. Conflict can be constructive

Conflict can range from mild disagreement to violent confrontation, and, especially in its stronger forms, can be extremely destructive. However, it would be a significant mistake not to recognize that, in the right circumstances and if handled skilfully and confidently, conflict can actually be constructive. This is because carefully controlled conflict can spur innovation, free people up from tramline thinking, generate considerable learning, provide opportunities for people who have previously been at loggerheads with one another to respect one another, allow us to see situations from new perspectives, and so on. Conflict can be understood to be like fire. If it is controlled and handled carefully, it can be very productive and helpful, but if allowed to go unchecked, can be enormously destructive, raging out of control and drawing in a wide range of people who get harmed in the process. Developing the skills of handling conflict effectively is therefore a very important basis for best practice in tackling problems.

12. Accept what you can't change

'Facticity' is the technical term for the things we cannot change, the things that are beyond our control. There will always be such things, and we have to get used to that. Some people have a problem because they tend to be defeatist. They accept things that they don't need to accept – they fail to recognize that there are steps they could take to address their problems. However, the problem I am talking about here is the opposite of that. It refers to situations where people know there is nothing they can do, but they try to do it anyway. For example, someone who is interviewed for a job, but is unsuccessful may not be willing to let go of this fact. They may rail and rage against their potential employer, as if they have done them a significant injustice, rather than accept that, in the interviewing panel's view, another candidate was better suited to the job. Not getting the job does not mean that you are a failure or that you are inadequate; it simply means you were not their first choice. Change what you can change, by all means, but railing against what you cannot change is a waste of time and energy and succeeds only in generating unnecessary bad feeling.

13. Everyone has 24 hours in their day

'I don't have enough time' is a commonly heard claim in busy workplaces, and there is certainly a great deal of evidence to show that time pressures are very significant for a high proportion of people these days. However, what we have to recognize is that everybody has the same amount of time – 24 hours in each day, seven days in each week and so on. It is not the amount of time available that distinguishes some people from others in terms of work pressures; rather, it is what we try to do with that time. If we try to do too much, we can end up spreading ourselves too thinly and end up being far less productive than we might otherwise have been if we had planned our use of time more strategically. Similarly, some people respond to high levels of pressure by burying themselves in their work and do not take time to step back, plan, set priorities or develop effective strategies for managing that level of pressure. They risk getting stuck in a 'hamster wheel' of relentless pressure that does not get them very far at all. Managing high levels of pressure is a very challenging enterprise, but we very much need to develop strategies for doing so and not allow ourselves to try to do the impossible by being unrealistic about what can be achieved in the time available – for example, by internalizing, or colluding with, other people's unrealistic expectations, rather than challenging them.

14. Don't let forms shape your practice

I have often encountered situations on training courses about report writing and record keeping where people say things like: 'We can't do that; the form won't let us'. Of course, forms are a way of recording and collating information and therefore have an important part to play. However, recognizing the value of forms and allowing them to dictate our work practice are two different things. If the forms help, that's great, but if they are framed in such a way that they are unhelpful, shouldn't we be changing the forms, rather than changing our practice to suit the form? So, an important question to ask is: How do we get a form changed? What are the feedback mechanisms we can use to let the appropriate people know that these tools (for that is what forms are) are not well suited to purpose and need to be revised? The effort required to do this could be well repaid by the progress made and is certainly a better alternative to allowing forms (rather than our professional knowledge and values) to shape our practice.

15. Question routines

Routines can be very helpful, as they enable us to deal with straightforward matters quickly, easily and efficiently. However, there are two potential problems with this. One is the danger of 'routinization', which is what happens when we overgeneralize and adopt a routine approach to non-routine situations – that is, we fail to distinguish between those situations that are simple enough to be dealt with in a routinized way and those that are not. The other danger is that routines become part of a culture and continue to be used long after the situation that first led to their development has ceased to apply. That is, they have become habits which were useful to begin with but are no longer helpful but continue to be used because no one has thought to do anything different. It is therefore important to question our routines from time to time, to see whether we are: (i) overextending them to non-routine situations; and/or (ii) still using routines that have long since lost their usefulness.

16. Make a note of important ideas

I regularly run courses on which, despite having been given handouts with space for notes about each part of the course, a high proportion of the participants will not write down a single word. Perhaps they all have photographic memories or maybe they believe that learning happens by magic – they just have to hear what is being said and don't need to remember it or apply it in any way; it will just automatically make them better at their jobs without any effort on their part. Similarly, many people have a good idea, don't write it down and later struggle to remember what their important insight was. I don't understand why so many people appear to be reluctant to make a note of important matters that come to their attention, but they are clearly losing out. So, do you have a system for making notes of important ideas and issues or are you happy to risk losing out by failing to learn from your experiences?

17. **Start your own book of the month club**

When I worked with students on a full-time basis, I would suggest that, once they went out into the big wide world as qualified professionals, they should make sure that they continued to learn and develop. In particular, I would urge them to continue to read about their profession and build up their knowledge base over time. I would suggest to them that they should buy a book every month when they received their salary payment, so that it became an established pattern for them. I have since met several of those ex-students who have told me that they did just that and were glad they did, as it helped them to not only keep learning, but also to retain a sense of professionalism, recognizing that their work is rooted in an important professional knowledge base. So, how do you make sure that you are continuing to learn and maintaining your sense of professionalism?

18. Why here? Why now?

When people come to us for help or reach the last straw when it becomes clear that they cannot continue without help, it can be very helpful to ask: Why here? Why now? In other words, it pays to be clear about what has made the difference between carrying on as before and seeking change. It is often the case that the problem(s) people need help with have been around for some time, but they have not sought help before. So, why now? What has been the key factor that has made the difference. The answer to that question may tell us a great deal about the situation, how it is perceived by the person(s) concerned and therefore what it means to them. It can also be helpful to ask: Why here? That is, why have they come to *you*? If there were other options available (and there usually are), why have they come here to seek your help? In some circumstances that too can cast important light on the subject. Failing to ask ourselves these questions can mean that we are missing out on important information.

19. Don't reply in anger

Anger is a powerful emotion, and one that no one is immune to. The physiological effect it has on us can be a strong spur to action, and so the temptation to respond there and then can be an intensely felt one. However, responding there and then can be highly problematic, as the intense emotion of the situation can distort our perceptions. It can also lead to an escalation in which our anger-driven response can 'up the stakes' emotionally and thereby lead to a worsening of the situation, rather than defuse it. In addition, it can mean that we are responding without a full understanding of the situation, and that could lead to making the situation worse. The traditional idea of 'count to 10' has some merit, but it is not enough on its own, as the effects of anger can last for some considerable time – for example, they can become resentment. Anger is a valid response to many situations, but we have to make sure that it is not allowed to create further problems or ill-feeling.

20. Say thank you

Saying please and thank you is a basic part of what we are taught as children. But saying thank you is more than just good manners. It is a way of showing appreciation and of cementing cooperative working relations. While it is certainly not uncommon for people to say thank you to one another in the appropriate circumstances, there are also very many occasions when it is not said and when it could have been very helpful to do so. There are also many times when it is said in a curt or routine way that does not really convey appreciation – it comes across as just a social ritual, rather than a meaningful (and effective) communication. Try two things as an exercise. First, watch carefully as people interact (whether in real life or on TV or in films) and note how often thank you is not said (or not said convincingly) and consider how different the interaction might have been if a genuine thank you had been said. Second, try saying thank you meaningfully whenever the opportunity arises (without going overboard!) and see what response you get from people.

21. Choose the right communication method

Email has proven to be a very effective communication tool, saving a great deal of time, money and effort compared with the pre-email days. However, email has also brought problems, not least the well-documented 'flame wars' where miscommunication upon miscommunication has produced a series of heated interchanges that would probably have never happened in face-to-face circumstances. One problem that has received far less attention is the tendency to overuse email, to use it as *the* tool of communication, rather than one amongst many. For example, some matters can be much better dealt with by a telephone conversation or even a face-to-face meeting. And, while email has replaced letters in many situations, there remain many circumstances where a letter is a better solution – for example, where an extra degree of formality is called for or in responding to serious concerns. So, while email is an excellent tool, we need to make sure that we don't allow it to take over and leave no room for other methods of getting our message across.

22. Clarify boundaries

Often confusion arises because there is a lack of clarity about who is responsible for what. The more pressurized the situation is, the more likely this problem is to occur. This confusion can breed anxiety, and that anxiety, in turn, can lead to fuzzy thinking which then contributes to confusion about boundaries. There is therefore much to be gained from being clear about where the boundaries lie. It is important to be clear about what you are personally responsible for in any given situation. But it is also important to be clear about what part you play in any shared responsibility. Are the others who share that responsibility clear about their contribution and are you all clear about how you are going to exercise your shared responsibility? Are you also clear about what is not your responsibility so that you can avoid stressing yourself out by worrying about matters that are someone else's responsibility? Establishing clarity about boundaries not only makes our own position easier to manage, it also provides a much firmer basis for working in partnership.

23. Live to fight another day

This is not literally about fighting. It is about recognizing when it is not appropriate to deal with a situation here and now. When there are concerns that need to be addressed or conflicts that need to be worked through, it is often helpful to be responsive to those demands at the time, rather than miss the opportunity to nip the problem in the bud. However, in some circumstances it is wiser not to react at the time – for example, situations where an immediate response may inflame the situation or encourage a defensive reaction. In such situations it can be more effective to arrange a more suitable time and place to raise your concerns or deal with the issues involved – one that is more conducive to constructive dialogue. But it is very important to make sure that you do find a suitable time and place. There is a fine line between this idea of 'living to fight another day' and copping out from raising what could be an awkward or uncomfortable matter to deal with. On one side of that line is a wise approach to problem solving, while on the other lies a failure to address an important concern.

24. **I-Thou, not I-it**

This distinction comes from the work of Buber, a theologian. I-Thou refers to interactions that are premised on dignity and mutual respect. These can be enriching and humanizing for both parties. I-it interactions, by contrast, are purely instrumental, purely about getting the job done with the minimum of human connection – not necessarily rude or discourteous, but with no warmth or feeling. These interactions can be dehumanizing not only for the person on the receiving end of such an approach, but also the person who initiates this type of interaction. Some people rely on I-it interactions because they have no motivation to rise above simply getting the job done. However, even people who are committed to I-Thou interactions and the advantages they bring can slide into I-it interactions at times – for example, when they are under high levels of pressure, are working in a context of low morale or have other concerns that are distracting them from doing their job to the best of their ability. This can be dangerous, as it can create a vicious circle: interacting with people at an I-it level can make us far less effective, potentially lead to complaints and/or dissatisfactions, bringing additional pressure which can then make it all the more likely that we respond to others in an I-it way.

25. Look for reasons, not causes

People commonly talk about what causes a particular behaviour or reaction. However, as it is people we are talking about, it makes more sense to talk about reasons, rather than causes. Human beings exist in a social context that is very powerful in its wide range of influences and we are, of course, subject to certain biological forces and constraints. But none of this removes human 'agency', to use the technical term, the ability to make choices. If we are looking for causes not reasons, we can be neglecting some key aspects of how a situation arose or how it is likely to unfold. For example, if I chose to make a complaint about a person or organization treating me disrespectfully, it may be said that being offended 'caused me to do so'. However, the reason I did so may have more to do with wanting to ensure other people do not have to endure such a bad experience than my feelings of being offended. Of course, it would be naïve not to recognize that we do not have *complete* control over our circumstances, but it would also be very unwise to assume that we have *no* control over what happens to us, that we are just passive victims of circumstance. To make sense of a complex situation, we need to understand both the influences on choices and the reasons for the choices actually made.

26. Dress for the part

'I should be able to wear what I want and not be judged' said one participant on a training course I was running. I agreed with her, particularly the word 'should', but I had to point out that people do attach significance to what we wear, even though ideally that should not happen. Our clothing is part of nonverbal communication. Whether we intend it or not, whether we agree with it or not, what we wear provides information about us that other people will generally attach significance to. For example, you may be highly committed to a job you are applying for, but if you turn up for the interview wearing jeans and a T-shirt, it is highly likely you will be seen to be conveying a lack of seriousness towards that job. But less extreme examples apply on a much more frequent basis, so it is important to ask ourselves: is my choice of clothing today conveying the message I want to put across to people? This does not mean that we should always dress formally, but it does mean we need to be tuned in to what message our clothes convey in different circumstances.

27. Use 'holding' emails

Email communication is a very strong feature of modern working life for a high proportion of people. It can be a very convenient and helpful form of communication, but it can also be highly problematic in a number of ways. One such way is the common (but thankfully not universal) expectation that responses will be more or less instant. This can lead to two sets of difficulties. One is that the person receiving an email may feel under pressure to reply there and then (when perhaps a more considered response would be wiser) and another is that the person sending the email can feel they are being ignored if they do not receive a prompt response. One way of addressing this problem is for the recipient to send a 'holding' message, something like: 'Thank you for your message. I will give the matter my careful consideration and come back to you as soon as I can'. This will prevent hurried ill-thought-through messages being sent and will also stop the sender sending follow up messages to see if their first message had been received. This technique also prevents us from feeling overwhelmed by email and therefore prone to getting stressed about it.

28. Don't try to do the impossible

The Avenue e-learning course, *Successful Time and Workload Management,* is based on four rules of time and workload management. One of those rules is: too much work is too much work. That is, if you have too much to do in the time available, then you need to find different ways of doing things rather than just try to do more than is possible and quite feasibly work yourself into a vicious circle in which your work pressures become increasingly unmanageable. A key word here is 'strategizing'. Don't try to do the impossible by trying to do two days' work every day. Use reflective practice to explore strategies for managing the pressures you face so that you are not overwhelmed by them. Strategizing won't provide magic answers, but it will certainly put you in a much stronger position than trying to do the impossible.

29. Take a break

Most workplaces seem to be very pressurized places these days. One of the dangers of this is that some people respond to pressures in ways that can make the situation worse. For example, it is not uncommon for busy people not to take a break. They seem to think that they are so busy that they just have to press on. But if we don't give our bodies and our minds the opportunity to recover from the strain we put them under in pressurized circumstances, we risk making ourselves ill through stress. We are also more likely to make mistakes, to be less creative, to fail to learn, to be more anxious and defensive in our practice, to gain less job satisfaction and ultimately burn ourselves out. It is only in exceptional circumstances that we should have to work through time that should be set aside for taking a break. If that is happening regularly, then either there is a fundamental issue around work overload that needs to be addressed or we are not being sufficiently disciplined in our self-care and we are allowing ourselves to risk being overstretched, with potentially serious consequences.

30. Use of self

We live in what seems to be an increasingly consumerist society where helping people seems to be interpreted mainly as giving them some sort of service. We seem to have lost sight of the well-established notion that the best resource we can offer people is ourselves – what textbooks have traditionally referred to as 'use of self'. By showing concern and interest and forging a meaningful human connection with people we can often be much more helpful to them than by referring them to a service which may or may not be of benefit to them. Some may argue that most people professionals don't have time to do that these days, but I would argue that, if you have the skills and confidence, it is possible to capitalize on 'use of self' in a relatively short period of time. It is in large part a matter of changing our mindset from a service delivery one to a problem-solving, empowerment one.

31. Try Garfinkeling

Harold Garfinkel made a name for himself as a sociologist by changing certain aspects of a social situation and seeing what the consequences would be. In this way, he was able to identify implicit social rules by breaking them. This process became known as Garfinkeling. An example would be to change the gender of a person in a certain situation (in order to highlight the gender role assumptions being made) and seeing what difference that makes. Changing age group can also be enlightening in terms of highlighting ageist assumptions. For example, I once came across a geriatrician who would challenge ageist statements by saying: 'Would you have made that comment if this person had been 30 years younger?'. Garfinkeling, then, is a useful tool for highlighting discriminatory assumptions by reversing some aspect of the situation so that previously taken-for-granted assumptions become apparent. Try it. It can be fun as well as enlightening.

32. Acknowledge problems, but focus on solutions

There tends to be a strong emphasis these days on 'positive thinking' and optimism. While there is much to be said for the benefits of such an approach, we also need to be aware of some of the dangers associated with it. One is for problems to be swept under the carpet in our desire to focus on the positive elements of a situation and thereby de-emphasize the negative or problematic aspects. What can be much more fruitful is to ensure that we acknowledge the problems we come across, but then adopt a positive approach by focusing on solutions. This is a matter of finding a constructive balance. On the one hand, it is dangerous to ignore problems in some misguided sense of positivity, but on the other it can make problems worse if people allow concerns about such problems to predominate – that is, if they wallow in the negativity problems can produce. Being positive about problem solving can give us the best of both worlds: we are not naively ignoring problems, but nor are we allowing their negativity to undermine us. Indeed, such a positive approach to problem solving is an important basis for empowerment, for supporting other people in resolving their own difficulties.

33. Respect cultural differences

The idea of cultural sensitivity is now a well-established one, but my experience has taught me that many people do not fully understand the implications of that. For example, many times I have come across people who assume that it applies only when dealing with somebody whose skin colour is different from one's own. In reality, it is much more complex than this, as there will generally be cultural differences that relate to class, region, profession or vocation, linguistic group and so on. Culture is a much broader and more inclusive concept than it is generally given credit for. Our own cultural backgrounds and experiences will have been a profound influence on who we are (our identity), our sense of where we fit in the world and where we are going (our spirituality). So often breakdowns of communication and other problems have their roots in one person seeing the situation from their own cultural standpoint, while one or more others see it from different cultural standpoints.

34. Aim for adult-adult

Transactional analysis, or TA for short, is now often seen as old-fashioned, but good ideas have a tendency to endure beyond fashion. TA teaches us that we should aim for interactions with others that are characterized as adult-adult (that is, based on mutual respect and consideration) rather than parent-child (based on dominance), parent-parent (a power battle) or child-child (neither person taking ownership of the situation). This is a very simple framework of understanding, but it can be very useful in a variety of circumstances. For example, supervision at work can be very effective and empowering when it is adult-adult, but can create resentment and distance when it is carried out on a parent-child basis. So, are you relating to people in an adult-adult way, as this is what is likely to bring out the best in both parties? Is someone behaving towards you in a parent-child way? If so, how can you influence the situation to make it a more effective adult-adult set of interactions?

35. Don't take it personally

In the people professions we will often come across people who are distressed, agitated or otherwise in a bad place. Often this will result in their being unkind or worse towards others, including ourselves – even though we may be doing our best to help and support them. They may swear at us, insult us or even physically attack us. Now, while such behaviour is not acceptable and should therefore not be condoned, we should also recognize that we would be wise not to take such matters personally. It is much more likely that they are taking their frustrations out on the role we occupy or the organization we represent or, ironically, may be venting their dismay and/or wrath in our direction because they feel safe enough with us to do so (a very backhanded compliment!). Encountering such negative feelings is difficult and challenging enough, so we have to make sure we do not make it worse by taking it personally when in most situations that is not likely to be the case.

36. Remove distractions where possible

Effectiveness in working with people relies to a large extent on being able to communicate successfully, to make a genuine and meaningful connection with the person(s) concerned. Distractions can get in the way of this (for example, a television being on during a home visit or noise coming from an adjacent room). We need to be tuned in to how problematic such distractions can be, and this is for two reasons. First, it makes it harder for both parties to 'connect' where there are distractions; and, second, if it is clear that you are aware of such distractions and you are doing nothing about it, both your credibility and your effectiveness go down significantly. So, having the presence of mind to identify distractions and the negotiation skills necessary to reduce or minimize them is an important foundation for good practice in the people professions. Sadly, I have seen so many people try to press on despite distractions and pay the price when it would have been far more effective to recognize the significance of the distraction and try to do something about it.

37. Use distractions where possible

In the previous tip I talked about how distractions can get in the way of effective communication, but in this one I want to look at how distracting someone can be a helpful thing to do in certain circumstances. It is a technique well known to many parents: to distract their child when they are misbehaving, getting upset or otherwise being demanding. But few people recognize that it can also work well with adults (provided that it is not done in a patronizing way). It can be useful when someone is anxious and/or fixated on a particular concern, depressed or agitated. It has to be done tactfully and sensitively, but it can make a very positive difference in the right circumstances. For example, if someone is focusing purely on the negatives of a situation, it can be helpful to try and balance this out by helping them to focus on the positive aspects of their circumstances.

38. Recognize warning signs of aggression and potential violence

There are some obvious signs of aggression and potential violence, such as reddening of the face, threatening gestures and so on. However, it is important to realize that there are many other, more subtle clues that can alert us to the potential for aggression and violence. In situations where we anticipate someone may become aggressive (where we have to deny their request, for example), we need to be using our nonverbal communication skills and watching carefully for signs that tension is growing. There is often an escalation. For example, it may start with something quite minor and normally imperceptible (drumming of fingers, moving about uneasily in their seat and so on). There are things we can do to minimize the chances of aggression and violence (effective listening, for example), but ultimately, if you feel you are in real danger of being assaulted it is wise to leave the situation at the earliest opportunity – for your own protection and also for their protection, as having a criminal assault charge against them is likely only to make their situation worse.

39. Use reframing

We all see the world in different ways, so my perspective may be different from yours. But what also happens is that people become comfortable with their way of seeing the world and can be reluctant to change it, even if such a change could actually improve their situation. 'Reframing' is the highly skilled process of helping someone see their situation from a different, more positive and empowering perspective. For example, if someone applies for a job, is interviewed but does not get the job, they may come to the conclusion that they were not good enough for that job and may be dissuaded from applying for similar jobs in future. However, helping them to see the situation differently (that is, reframing it) can be very helpful, helping them to understand that it is more likely that they were plenty good enough for that job, it's just that on the day the interviewers felt that someone else had more to offer at that point in time. Many people's tendency to see the world in a self-defeating or self-disempowering ways is sadly a common feature of working in the people professions, and so reframing can be extremely helpful at times.

40. **Avoid rumination**

When we experience powerful negative emotions, such as when we are grieving, upset, angry or disappointed, they can dominate our thinking for a while. We find it difficult to push them to the back of our mind and try to get past them. But normally we will do so sooner or later. However, what can happen sometimes is that we get locked into a cycle of negativity. We can 'ruminate'. This means that we go over and over things in our mind; we find it difficult to stop coming back to what has hurt us. This is to be expected in the early aftermath of a difficult experience, but it can continue for weeks, months or even years, constantly sapping our energy and disempowering us. So, it is important to recognize the dangers of rumination – in ourselves and others. Where this 'locking in' to a cycle of negativity has occurred we need to look carefully at strategies for breaking out of it.

41. Failure is part of success

We tend to see failure as the opposite of success. But this simplistic way of viewing failure hides some very complex issues. It is more accurate and realistic to think of failure as part of success. A one hundred per cent success rate in any significant project is relatively rare. Most of the time, success encompasses failure. Sometimes, it is failing at one thing that enables us to succeed at something else – for example, by seeing where we have been going wrong, what assumptions we have been making that need to change. Furthermore, fear of failure can be a major obstacle to innovation, to a balanced approach to risk and to learning. And, let's be clear about it, we fail on a regular basis. Every time we do a typo, we 'failed' to get it right first time; every time we are a minute late for a meeting, we 'failed' to get there on time; and so on. Failure is not just the opposite of success, so we need to make sure that we do not allow a simplistic understanding of failure to stand as an obstacle to success.

42. Don't be a rescuer

In conflict situations it is not uncommon for one or more parties to feel that they are being persecuted, that they are being treated unfairly. This is often due to the conflict concerned revolving around different perceptions of the situation. For example, where there are two people in conflict it is very common for each to perceive the other as being 'difficult' or 'awkward' – that is, each seeing the situation in personal, rather than interpersonal, terms. Where this occurs the result can be what is known as the 'drama triangle'. This is where one person in the conflict (who plays the role of victim) draws in a third party to seek support (to be a rescuer) against the other party who is cast as the persecutor. If you are that third party and you allow yourself to be seduced into being a rescuer, you may then find yourself in difficulty when you discover that the alleged persecutor sees him- or herself as the victim and seeks to cast the other party as the persecutor. So, whenever you are called upon to 'rescue' someone from a difficult situation, first look at that situation carefully and particularly at any elements of conflict.

43. Don't speak (or write) officialese

The level of formality at which we speak or write is known technically as the 'register'. Sometimes it is appropriate to communicate fairly informally (informal register), while at others a more formal register is what is needed. However, some people confuse formal register with officialese. Perhaps this is a confidence issue: feeling not very confident about using a formal register may lead to stilted language use. Officialese is a style of language that is full of clichés and jargon terms and is unnecessarily convoluted. It is the opposite of plain language. It is perfectly possible to write formally within the bounds of plain language without resorting to officialese. In any form of communication, the major emphasis needs to be on clarity: am I getting across the point(s) I need to? Officialese stands in the way of clarity and is therefore no substitute for formal but clear language.

44. Set out your stall

If you are skilful at engaging with people and winning their trust, convincing them that you are a helpful and reliable person there is a danger that they will come to rely on you more and more and bring more and more of their problems and concerns to you. This can easily lead to you being overloaded, stretching yourself too thinly and potentially getting yourself into difficulties. So, it is important to be clear about what we can help with and what we can't – to 'set out our stall', as it were. If we lose sight of the boundaries of our role and become a general helper, it can be confusing all round. It can also prove stressful, as it means we have no control over our workload – the demand can be potentially infinite if people start bringing to us issues and concerns that are not part of our remit. The ability to be effective in negotiating expectations (making it clear where our role begins and ends and sticking to it) can be difficult at times, but it remains an important skill to have if we are not to allow ourselves to be pulled in all directions.

45. Keep your records up to date

There is a general expectation that professionals should keep a record of their work. Such records can often be assigned a secondary role and dismissed as relatively unimportant – just the 'paperwork'. Although this is understandable, we also have to bear in mind that record keeping is a form of professional communication – the absence of which can at times be potentially disastrous. What can easily happen is that a vicious circle can develop: record keeping is put off so that, by the time the professional concerned gets round to getting records up to date, there is an annoying and energy-sapping backlog. Dealing with a backlog of 'boring records' can demotivate us and make it even harder to keep up. What also contributes to the vicious circle is that the bigger the gap between the work being undertaken and the record of it being made, the harder it is to remember the details of what happened and the greater the risk of inaccuracies and mistakes (and the longer it takes to do the records if we are racking our brains trying to remember the details). So, all in all, there is much to be gained from developing a system and pattern of work that enables us to keep our records up to date and to avoid the problems that can ensue if we don't.

46. Need to know not nice to know

Gathering appropriate information to get a helpful picture of the situation we are dealing with is a central part of the role of a wide range of professionals. If we do not have a reasonably clear picture of the circumstances we are engaging with we can miss significant issues, distort and oversimplify the situation and potentially make a bad situations worse. Not having enough information can therefore be problematic. However, what can also be problematic is if we have too much information. This is because: (i) we can waste a lot of time and effort in gathering more information than we need; (ii) we can confuse ourselves and others if we end up drowning in far more information than is necessary for our purposes; (iii) important information can get lost in the welter of more details than are helpful; and (iv) we may alienate people if they feel we are putting together a fuller dossier of information than the current situation requires. So, the key skill here is being able to keep very focused on our role and task so that we know what is relevant information and what is not.

47. Fail to plan and you plan to fail

This is one of those tips that sounds so obvious and straightforward and yet is one that is so badly needed, given how often people seem to manage to get themselves into difficulties by either not planning at all or not planning fully enough. In working with people there are so many unpredictable variables but there is also much that can be anticipated if we take the trouble to think ahead and draw on our professional knowledge in the process. There is a great irony that people often say they are too busy to plan, whereas in reality it is more likely to be the case that a lack of planning could well be part of the reason why they are so busy. Planning need not take very long, but the time and effort it can save can be extremely worthwhile, as can the increased effectiveness, motivation, learning and credibility – all of which are recognized benefits of planning.

48. Apologize where necessary

Some people seem to think that an apology is an admission of guilt or even of negligence and are therefore very careful not to utter the word 'sorry'. This is very unfortunate, as saying sorry can defuse a tense situation, while not saying sorry when an apology could have helped a great deal can inflame a situation quite significantly. But often it isn't a deliberate strategy to withhold an apology; it's simply a matter of allowing work pressures to distract us to the extent that we lose sight of basic manners. Our own pressures stop us from seeing the situation from the other person's point of view and thereby prevent us from taking their feelings into account. A classic example of this is when a complaint is made about something of low to medium importance, evokes an unapologetic response which is interpreted as being 'fobbed off', which then leads to a much stronger complaint being made – a deeper hole has been dug, and totally unnecessarily.

49. Save face

To lose face means to become embarrassed or to feel that your standing has been diminished. Unfortunately, if we are not sensitive enough in our interactions with other people, we can easily unintentionally make them lose face – for example, by implying a criticism of them. In some cases this can lead you an aggressive reaction. This is because, if people are faced with a choice between losing face and reacting strongly, many will choose the latter. Indeed, feeling diminished or humiliated is a common cause of aggressive or even violent reactions. We therefore need to make sure that we are skilful enough to avoid contributing to situations where people lose face. Saving face means, on the one hand, not embarrassing ourselves, but also making sure we don't unwittingly embarrass anyone else. This is partly basic good manners, but it is also about being able to tune in to the situation we find ourselves in and being alert to any potential sources of losing face. For example, in circumstances where someone is, or has been, upset or angry, they are more likely to regard an ill-chosen comment as a slight. This does not mean that we should be 'walking on eggshells', but it does mean that we may create problems if we just press on without considering the dangers of causing someone to lose face.

50. Tune in to grief

The idea that 'grief is the price we pay for love' is a longstanding one. When we love (a person, a thing, a job or whatever) we may make an emotional commitment or investment ('cathexis', to use the technical term). When we lose who or what we have invested in we feel the emptiness of the emotional void that has been created by that loss. This can affect us at different levels (physically, mentally, emotionally, socially and spiritually) and can have a hugely powerful impact on our lives. Some people make the mistake of assuming that grief applies only to death, but, of course, it can arise as a result of any significant loss. If we make the mistake of not taking account of grief in people's lives, we can be basing our actions and interactions on a very partial and distorted picture of the situation.

51. Be prepared for meetings

I have run very many training courses where I have asked the group: 'How many of you prepare for meetings so that you are better equipped to get the best results from the time you are putting in?'. It is very rare for the majority of responses to be in the affirmative and quite often it is as little as 10% or so of the group. And yet, if you think about it, many people spend a great deal of time in meetings, much of which can be wasted, unproductive (if not counterproductive) time if it is not focused enough. It can therefore be helpful to do some pre-meeting preparation by asking yourself: (i) What do I want out of this meeting?; and (ii) What do I want or need to put into it? It may then be that, in some circumstances, you will decide that there is little point in attending. However, where you do attend you should be in a stronger position to gain some benefit from your attendance if you are clear about what you want to contribute and what you want to take from the meeting.

52. Manage your own learning

It is now increasingly being appreciated that self-directed learning is the most effective form of learning. That is, if we are able to identify for ourselves what we want or need to learn and how we are going to learn it, we are likely to be more motivated and the learning gained will be more suited to our own specific needs. Unfortunately, though, many people adopt a passive approach to learning – they assume that it is someone else's job to take the lead, an 'expert' in learning like a teacher, tutor, trainer or mentor. Of course, such people can be very helpful as guides, advisers, sources of encouragement, support and ideas, but the more control we have over our own learning, the more effective it is likely to be – and the more committed we will be to continuing to learn throughout our careers. Teachers, tutors, trainers and mentors can often provide helpful maps of the learning territory, but we need to determine our own itinerary if we are to get the best results

53. Compartmentalize home and work

How to manage a range of pressures is a challenge that we all face. A very worrying (but sadly not uncommon) scenario is when we allow home and work pressures to combine to overwhelm our coping resources. An alternative strategy is that of 'compartmentalization'. This means training ourselves to focus on our home pressures when we are at home and our work pressures when we are at work and having a clear boundary between the two. Many people achieve this by having some sort of ritual that symbolizes the end of the working day and the return to home life – for example, by getting changed. Different rituals work for different people, but they can all play an important role in keeping our two domains separate so that we do not find ourselves in the situation where home and work pressures combine to leave us feeling stressed and ill-equipped to cope with the challenges we face.

54. Use touch appropriately

Physical contact is a very powerful form of communication. It can be powerfully negative – for example, touch used in a threatening or aggressive way or as an invasion of privacy – or powerfully positive as a means of conveying support, concern, affirmation and validation. Provided that we have the sensitivity to know where the boundary is between supportive and intrusive touch, we can use touch to express empathy and concern, build trust and make an important contribution to helping people who are facing considerable challenges or who would benefit from human connection at a time of difficulty. Do you know of anyone who uses touch very sensitively and effectively? Watch them closely when you can and see what you can learn from how they use it.

55. Why helps with how

In any project or task we undertake, it can be very easy to get engrossed and lose focus on why we are doing it. If, however, we can make sure we don't lose sight of the why (the purpose), we will be in a stronger position to decide on the how (the method) and put it into practice. Sadly, though, it is not uncommon for people to become so busy doing something that they forget why they are doing it. They then lose sight of how best to move forward. Clarity about why we are doing something will make us more motivated to achieve our goals and give us a more helpful picture of the possible ways of achieving them. If other people involved in the situation are clear about why we are doing something, then they will be in a stronger position to play their part in making the project a success.

56. Be open to learning from mistakes

The idea of the value of learning from our mistakes is well established, but unfortunately many people don't manage to get the benefit of this. That is because they adopt a defensive approach to mistakes; they see them as things to cover up or deflect attention from. Nobody is perfect and so mistakes are inevitable, therefore there is little point in trying to give the impression that we never make mistakes. Some mistakes can be embarrassing, but most are not, unless we are trying to come across as 'mistake proof'. Some mistakes are quite serious, but the more serious they are, the greater the scope for learning. However, that's not to say that even small mistakes cannot produce significant learning. But, of course, no mistake will produce learning unless we are prepared to be open to learning by admitting that we are not perfect.

57. Make best use of your best time

Some people are morning people and some people are definitely not morning people. We all have our rhythms and routines that mean that we are at our best at certain times of day and far from our best at others. So, do you know when your best time of day is? If so, are you making sure that you are doing your most important work at that time of day in order to produce the best results? If not, why not try and work out when that is so that you can capitalize on it? Similarly, are you clear about when your least effective time is? If so, are you making sure that you are not making important decisions or carrying out vitally important tasks at those times? Understanding your best and worst times is an important part of self-awareness.

58. Allow time for recovery

Our muscles need time to recover form exertion before we exert ourselves further if we are not to strain them. The same applies to our mental and emotional 'muscles'. If we keep stretching ourselves in our work efforts (and in our lives more broadly) without giving ourselves time to recover, we run the risk of doing ourselves harm, potentially significant harm. Exertion plus recovery plus more exertion can produce growth and development (of muscles in the direct physical sense or of learning in our more metaphorical sense). Exertion followed by more exertion without recovery time in between can produce muscle strain and/or psychological stress. Time for recovery is therefore not an optional extra if we are to take our physical and mental health seriously.

59. There's no point rushing

'More haste less speed' is a well-known saying and it has more than a grain of truth to it. So many people tend to respond to pressure by rushing, and this is a dangerously counterproductive strategy. When we rush our error rate goes up significantly and our sense of control goes down significantly – and, of course, losing our sense of control is a major step in the direction of stress. What is also significant is that, when we start rushing, we start giving people the message that they are not important, that we have more pressing things to do than to listen to them and take an interest in them. Working slightly faster than usual is one thing, rushing is quite another. If we find ourselves in a position where we feel the need to rush, that is the time to start reordering our priorities – taking our thinking up a gear, rather than letting it go down a gear by rushing.

60. Negotiate your workload

As I mentioned earlier, my *Successful Time and Workload Management* e-learning course emphasizes that too much work is too much work – that is, everyone has a limit to how much they can get done in a given timeframe. However, some people get themselves into difficulties by taking on everything that comes their way. They feel obliged to say yes to everything even if this means they may become overloaded to the point that they risk becoming stressed and possibly practising dangerously because of that. A key skill, then, is being able to successfully negotiate our workload. If we take on more than we can reasonably cope with, then we are likely to achieve far less than if we had kept our workload within manageable limits, and we also risk things going tragically wrong. Some people find it very difficult to be assertive about their workload limits, but allowing ourselves to get into that dangerous overload zone is very unwise.

61. Boundaries of responsibility

There are some things that each one of us is responsible for – that is, they are individual responsibilities. I have to do what I have to do and you have to do what you have to do. Some things are shared responsibilities – that is, we have to do them together. Teamwork is a good example of this. Developing effective teamwork is the responsibility of every team member, not just the leader. Then there are also responsibilities that belong to other people – they are not mine, they are not yours, they are not ours. It is important to be aware of these boundaries as it can be quite problematic and potentially stressful if: (i) we do not fulfil our individual responsibilities; (ii) we do not contribute to our shared responsibilities; or (iii) we overload ourselves by taking on responsibilities that are not ours, that belong elsewhere. The detrimental consequences of losing sight of these boundaries can be quite significant.

62. Get the information you need

Over the years I have come across many decisions that have proven after the event to have been unwise of misguided. There is no single reason for this, but a common theme has been people making decisions without having the information they need. Often what happens is that there is pressure to make a decision quickly and this can lead people into moving forward with their plans too soon because key elements of information were not available at the time the decision was made. So, in making any decision we have to be clear about which is wiser: deciding now without that information and risking getting it wrong, or take the time to find out – thereby making a much sounder decision – but risking causing problems associated with the delay involved. Unless there are reasons why we need to make the decision very soon, it is generally wiser to get the information we need before deciding on our course of action.

63. Don't allow other people's pressures to distort your priorities

It is important not to feel under pressure to dance to someone else's tune. For example, something seen as urgent by someone else does not necessarily mean you have to change your own priorities to accommodate it. This does not mean that we should not help people who need something doing urgently, but it does mean that the fact that something is urgent for somebody else should not be allowed to distort your own priorities. Sadly, I have come across many situations where Person A has something urgent (but not especially important) that they want Person B to do and, when Person B does it, the result is that something much more important from Person B's own to do list does not get done – often with more serious consequences than if Person A's task had not been done. By all means take requests for urgent help seriously, but don't make the mistake of assuming that you have to oblige if that means you are creating potentially worse problems than you are solving.

64. Assess, don't assume

In many aspects of the people professions we are called upon to assess situations, weigh them up as part of making a decision as to how to deal with them. This is skilful work that can be helped by having a good working knowledge base around people (about motivation, for example). But what is not helpful is the tendency to rely on untested assumptions. At one extreme, this can amount to relying on stereotypes, crude caricatures that present a heavily distorted picture. But we can also encounter more subtle distortions, mainly based on the assumption that other people see the world the way we do. For example, something we see as simple and straightforward may be quite scary and disconcerting to someone else. It is therefore important that we make the effort to develop a more holistic picture, taking account of other people's perspectives and checking things out where necessary rather than taking things for granted and potentially producing an inaccurate and unhelpful picture of the situation.

65. Values are not set in stone

Values are, of course, a key factor when it comes to working with people. Values shape our (and other people's) thoughts, feelings and actions. However, we have to be careful not to oversimplify the situation in relation to values; we should not allow them to become fixed and rigid and dogmatically apply them across the board when perhaps a more nuanced approach is called for. For example, there can be clashes between different sets of values that can be difficult to reconcile. Critically reflective practice means that we need to have a flexible approach to our knowledge base – and much the same can be said to apply to our value base. At one unhelpful extreme we have a lack of integrity by which I mean a significant gap between espoused values and actual actions taken. But at the other extreme we can have a dogmatic approach to values that does not do justice to the complexities involved. Critically reflective practice helps us to find the healthy balance between the two.

66. Don't get too comfortable

It can feel really good to be comfortable, to be out of danger, with no significant hassles at that particular time. So, it can be very appealing to enter what is often called the 'comfort zone'. But, ironically, there are dangers involved in getting too comfortable, in being too keen to stay in that warm and cosy place. It can stop us learning; discourage us from being imaginative and creative and thereby block innovation; and at times it can also make us complacent. So, rather than get too used to our comfort zone, perhaps we should think of it as somewhere we return to as a safe haven after we have allowed ourselves to go beyond it and be a bit more adventurous in our dealings with the world. Too much of a good thing can be bad for you, and comfort is something that can come under that heading too. If we never venture beyond our comfort zone, it becomes a cage, rather than a home.

67. Put yourself in their shoes

Many a problem has been caused by someone putting something in writing in a way that led to misunderstanding. What you intended to convey and what is interpreted by the reader can sometimes be very different indeed. For example, what you intended to be friendly advice could be perceived as issuing instructions. These mismatches arise because communication does not take place in a vacuum. When you write something you will be doing so within a context of your own circumstances and your own frameworks of meaning. The person reading what you have written will be doing so within their own context and their own frameworks of meaning, and so there is plenty of scope for misunderstanding. What can be helpful is this: if you are writing a letter or report, imagine you are the intended recipient and have just opened and read it. That is, put yourself in the recipient's shoes. Are you sure, when you look at it from this perspective, that what you have written will convey what you wanted it to?

68. Don't assume you can't make a difference

Sometimes the difficulties we face in organizations can seem so deep rooted and so extensive that we can feel there is nothing that can be done about them. A pervasive sense of defeatism and hopelessness can easily set in. This is especially the case where morale is low. The result can be a vicious circle: defeatism contributes to low morale and low morale makes people feel helpless. In reality there is often much that individuals can do – especially when working collectively – to make a positive difference. Organizational cultures – whether positive or negative – are basically sets of habits, and habits can be changed. Start to explore possibilities, rather than assume that there aren't any.

69. The importance of feedback

If you are not successful at an interview or a promotion panel you may feel so disappointed that you just want to put it behind you. You may feel too 'raw' to ask for constructive feedback, but it is well worth getting past this as that feedback could be extremely helpful in giving you guidance on how to learn from the experience and improve for next time. Without that guidance you may be making the same mistake next time and the time after that, which could be very destructive of your confidence and self-esteem. Learning from feedback is an important part of continuous professional development.

70. Perspective taking

We get so used to seeing the world from our own point of view that it is easy to forget that how other people see it can be very different. For example, what is routine and straightforward to you can be quite scary and unsettling to someone else who does not have the experience of that type of situation that you have. So, it is important at all times to remember that other people are not inside your head with you – we need to be careful not to be 'egocentric' by assuming that our 'take' on the situation is the only way to see it. The idea of perspective taking is that of putting ourselves in the other person's shoes as far as possible. This can come from a mixture of imagining how they might be feeling and actually checking out with them what their perspective is.

71. Focus on what motivates

When we need to make changes in our lives we can sometimes find it difficult to motivate ourselves. This is often because we tend to focus on what we need to do to achieve the desired change rather than on the change itself. For example, if you want to lose weight, focusing on eating less and/or exercising may seem like a bind, something you are reluctant to engage in. However, if you focus on weight loss and the benefits it would bring, you are far more likely to feel motivated to make the changes. This may seem simple, obvious even, but that doesn't alter the fact that so many people continue to focus on means rather than the ends and thereby demotivate themselves. The same logic applies to not only motivating ourselves, but also to helping others to motivate themselves.

72. Define the problem

Are you looking for a solution without really knowing what the problem is? Very often we can find ourselves in a pressurized situation where there is a strong sense that 'something must be done'. If we are not careful that pressure can lead us to trying out solutions without really knowing what the problem is. Sometimes we will get lucky and we will be able to resolve the situation purely by chance, in the sense that our ill-defined 'solutions' just happen to address our ill-defined problems. However, what is much more likely is that we will make little progress by being so unfocused and may, at times, actually make the situation worse. So, it's important that we spend some time and effort in trying to define what the problem is before we try and come up with ways of dealing with it. This is an important aspect of reflective practice.

73. Be prepared for conflict

There is a common misperception of conflict. It tends to be assumed that everyday reality is basically harmonious and conflict is an exception – conflict 'breaks out' to shatter the normality of harmony. However, we don't need to pay much close attention to what actually happens to realize that, in fact, conflict is an everyday occurrence. Day-to-day reality is a mixture of harmony and conflict. We learn basic conflict management skills as we grow up, and so we have a good foundation on which to build so that we can take our skills to a more advanced level and become more confident and competent in dealing with those situations in which conflict starts to escalate. Continuing to see conflict as somehow abnormal leaves us ill-equipped to rise to some of the more challenging aspects of conflict.

74. Complain to the right person

Sadly, it is often the case these days that we feel the need to make a complaint. What is even sadder is that so many organizations seem ill-equipped to respond positively to people's concerns – and that can lead to considerable ill feeling and an intensification of pressures. What can make such situations even worse is when the complaint is made to someone who cannot do anything about it (and who is perhaps not inclined to pass the concerns on to someone who can). So, whenever you need to make a complaint, make sure that you complain to the person or body that has the power to do something to address the problem. Working out who that is may not always be easy, but it saves an awful lot of frustration compared with raising issues with people who are not well placed to solve the problem.

75. Hear the silence

The importance of listening is well established, but what is often not realized that the most effective form of listening involves paying attention to what someone is *not* saying, as well as what they *are* saying. Just as silence is an important part of music, working out what is not being said is a key part of genuinely connecting with people, of forming an effective rapport. To hear what is not being said involves tuning in to the situation, considering the context, the emotions involved, where the conversation is coming from and where it is going. These are quite advanced skills, but they can be developed over time.

76. Projects are gardens not buildings

A common way of thinking about projects is to conceive of them as buildings, something you construct and then have in place to serve you in whatever way the project was intended to. Despite this being a normal way of understanding projects, it is actually a misleading oversimplification. This is because whatever project you work on will not remain static or unchanging. A more accurate and helpful way of understanding projects is to see them as gardens – that is, as things that need to be tended, nurtured, pruned from time to time and not allowed to get overgrown. So, whatever projects you are involved in, you need to ask yourself: am I treating it as a building or as a garden?

77. Don't assume you are wrong

Some people can be quite dogmatic and stick to their views despite evidence and argument to the contrary, and that of course is not helpful. However, it can also be problematic when some people go to the opposite extreme and simply assume that they are wrong whenever they encounter any resistance or disagreement. What is needed, of course, is a balanced approach. Being dogmatic does not help, but nor does abandoning your views prematurely. Being open minded is essential, but that need to include being open to the possibility that you were right all along.

78. Accept what you can't change

There are things that we can change directly, things that we can change indirectly (through influence), but there are very many things that we cannot change at all. When we encounter these we basically have two choices: (i) we can learn to accept that we cannot bring about change, make the best of the situation and invest our energies in those things we can change; or (ii) waste a lot of time and energy trying to do the impossible and/or become negative, defeatist or even cynical about the fact that there are certain things we cannot change. Which option we choose will have major consequences for ourselves, our colleagues and the people we are seeking to help. So, make sure you choose wisely.

79. Cultivate self-awareness

Self-awareness is an important basis for reflective practice. It involves being able to tune in to: (i) what effect you are having on the situation; and (ii) what effect the situation is having on you. When we interact with other people, we become part of that dynamic; we shape the situation to a certain extent, and so we will be in a stronger position to influence that situation in a positive direction if we are aware of what effect our presence and contribution are having. It is also helpful to be aware of what effect the situation is having on us: Are we anxious? Are we rushing? Are we tired? All these things can have a significant bearing on how the interaction develops, so we would do well to be alert to what part they are playing in shaping the dynamic.

80. Don't reinvent the wheel

We can so easily become so engrossed in our work and under so much pressure that we don't look more broadly at the situation we are dealing with. This can mean that we can find ourselves reinventing the wheel – that is, not realizing that it is likely that other people will have faced the type of situation we are in now and will have found helpful ways of responding to it. There is much to be learned from finding out how other people tackle their challenges, but we won't do any of that learning if we don't take the trouble to try and find out. If we don't make that effort, we will be doomed to reinvent the wheel and not learn from other people's experiences.

81. Practise self-leadership

A key part of leadership is being able to work with a group to establish where they are heading for and help them get there. Are you clear about where you want to get to and how you are going to get there? Having this sense of direction is an important pat of spirituality and can be a great personal resource. We may wander aimlessly without it.

82. More is not necessarily better

In our consumerist society we constantly find ourselves under pressure to earn more, buy more, achieve more. So much these days seems to depend on quantity, with relatively little attention being paid to quality, particularly quality of life. The idea that 'more is not necessarily better' is not only something to bear in mind for ourselves and our own well-being, but also for the people we are trying to help or support. While there is much that can be done to help people who are lacking in material resources, we should not lose sight of the fact that there should also be ways in which we can help people enrich their lives in other ways.

83. Elegant challenging

When people act or speak in discriminatory ways, bully people or behave disrespectfully towards others, it can be very tempting to 'have a go' at them, to give them a piece of your mind. While that reaction is quite understandable, it can be highly problematic. This is because there is a danger that the person who is behaving irresponsibly will see you as the unreasonable one, to see you as the person who is behaving inappropriately. This can just make a difficult situation worse. 'Elegant' challenging, by contrast, refers to challenging inappropriate behaviour tactfully and sensitively, so that you are giving the other person no ammunition to fire back at you. Skilfully pointing out why what somebody has said or done is problematic is much less likely to produce a defensive response and is therefore much more likely to be effective.

84. Make it happen – carpe diem

In today's busy, pressurized world we can find ourselves with many different demands on our time. As a result of this, important things may not get done. We can find ourselves drifting and losing sight of what is important to us. 'Carpe diem' – seize the day – is a good principle to guard against that. It can pay huge dividends to step back from time to time, to clarify what matters to us and focus on making happen whatever needs to happen to make sure those important things are given the attention they deserve.

85. Direct concerns to where the power is

A phenomenon I have come across many times in many organizations is for matters of dissatisfaction to act as a basis for moaning sessions (which do little good) and for the concerns or dissatisfactions not to be channelled in the direction of a person or group who can potentially do something about the problem. There is often a fear that if issues are raised the person(s) raising them will be seen as troublemakers, but it all depends on how the issues are raised. If they are raised in a confrontational approach, don't be surprised if the response is a defensive one (and some people, of course, will act on the basis that attack is the best form of defence). Raising concerns sensibly and sensitively with the people who have the power to do something about it will do far more good than just feeding low morale by moaning.

86. Develop an internal locus of control

Are you living your life or is your life living you? How much in control do you feel about what is happening to you? People who have what psychologists call an internal locus of control will have a good sense of being able to control (or at least influence) key aspects of their lives, both at work and at home. Someone with an external locus of control, by contrast, tends to have little sense of control and can pay a price for that in terms of lower confidence, higher stress levels and so on. In a very real sense, having an external locus of control is a form of self-disempowerment, a way of putting obstacles in your own way. So, it is important to be clear about what you can control and make things happen accordingly, rather than surrender to being a passive victim of circumstance.

87. Begin with the end in mind

This is one of Stephen Covey's seven secrets of highly effective people (Covey, 1999). It means that, at all times, we need to be clear about what we are trying to achieve or where it is we are trying to get to. Without that clarity we can drift and become unfocused. This is likely to hamper progress and can also prove stressful at times, as the lack of a sense of direction can create anxiety and uncertainty. It can also reduce our credibility (and thus our ability to influence other people) as we will come across in ways that do not inspire confidence if we are unfocused and unclear about what we are trying to achieve. Beginning with the end in mind is therefore wise counsel.

88. Capitalize on crisis

A crisis is a turning point in someone's life, a situation that will either get better or get worse. By definition, if it stays the same it is not a crisis. What can be a strong temptation when working with someone who is in crisis is to try and get things back to normal as soon as possible. While this is perfectly understandable, we have to recognize that this means that the positive potential of crisis is being missed. Crises can do a lot of harm (the situation gets worse) but they can also do a lot of good (the situation gets better) – for example, when new coping skills are learned, when longstanding obstacles to progress are removed and/or a renewed determination to move things forward is generated by the crisis situation. Crisis situations have to be handled very carefully and sensitively, but that does not mean that we cannot help people grow and develop by capitalizing on the positive potential.

89. Beware of cloning

The importance of valuing and even celebrating diversity is now well established, but what is often not appreciated is that the process of 'cloning' can stand in its way. What this refers to is the tendency to feel more comfortable with people who are 'like us' ('homophilia' is the technical term), so, if we ae not careful, we can find ourselves treading the same beaten path of relating to people similar to ourselves and thereby not getting the benefits of diversity and the enrichment it brings. For example, many businesses have suffered or even perished because they recruited 'people like us' and thereby developed a very narrow perspective that stood in the way of creative thinking, innovation and the ability to survive and thrive in a changing environment. Cloning is therefore the term used to refer to this unfortunate process of unwittingly excluding opportunities to capitalize on diversity.

90. Step back from time to time

Busy people can easily get themselves into a whirl of activity that strongly resembles a hamster wheel – an awful lot of energy being expended, but not necessarily much progress being achieved. What can therefore be of great value is to take a step back from time to time and think about what our current pressures are and work out what is the best way of dealing with them. Can we change anything in the way things are currently working out? Can we deal with certain issues differently to ease or remove certain pressure points? Can we reschedule or reprioritize certain things? Do we need someone's assistance or support in some areas? All these important questions can remain unanswered if we just press on and not make the time to step back and take stock. This is a key part of reflective practice.

91. Choose your time and place

Sometimes there are sensitive issues that need to be addressed – for example, pointing out to someone that their behaviour is causing you (or others) problems or is contrary to law or policy. Bringing this to their attention in front of other people or when feelings are running high (if their behaviour has caused annoyance, for example) can mean that they lose face and can feel 'got at'. This can not only make the situation worse by antagonizing them, but could also potentially lead to a complaint of bullying, on the grounds that your behaviour was humiliating and contrary to their dignity. It is important not to shy away from sensitive issues, but we do have to make sure that we deal with them in the right place and at the right time.

92. Believe in yourself

Confidence is not something that you either have or do not have or have in a certain quantity. Confidence is an attitude. The word confidence means 'trust', so whether you are confident or not depends on whether you trust yourself. Sadly, many people have little trust in themselves, little self-belief, and so they will approach new situations and challenges with an attitude that says: 'I can't do this'. People who believe in themselves, by contrast, will approach new situations with the attitude: 'I don't know whether I can do this, but I am going to have a damn good try'. That is, they do not write themselves off.

93. Give yourself thinking time

As we have noted, the modern workplace tends to be a pressurized one. There is therefore a temptation to just press on, to adopt an attitude of 'Head down, get on with it'. This can be highly dangerous as it means that people are making decisions, interacting with other people and generally going about their business without giving enough thought to what is involved or how it might go wrong. Part of the problem is that some workplace cultures can encourage this sort of behaviour and create the impression that stopping to think is a luxury you can't afford if you work here (rather than a necessity if you are to practise safely). So, whether the impetus to just 'Get on with the job' without thinking is coming from within yourself or from your wrong environment, the significant (and potentially disastrous) dangers remain the same.

94. Invest time to save time (sharpen your axe)

I mentioned earlier that the Avenue *Successful Time and Workload Management* e-learning course is based on four principles of time and workload management. One of those principles is 'Invest time to save time'. Unfortunately, busy people often fail to do this. There may be useful ways in which they could save time and energy, be more effective and/or achieve better results with the same resources, but many people will not explore these because they see themselves as being too busy to do so. That is, they don't invest time to save time. An investment is not the same as a cost – the idea is that you should get that time back, with interest. Abraham Lincoln is attributed with saying that, if he had six hours to chop down a tree, he would spend the first four sharpening the axe.

95. Think before you write

Jobs that involve working with people generally have a written work component to them (report writing and record keeping, for example). This can become a routine part of the job, and so there is a danger that we write without first thinking about what we are writing, why we are writing it and who we are writing it for. The result can be very poor-quality written work, communication breakdowns and misleading records and reports that have the potential to wreak havoc. What we write may continue to be used for many years to come by other people involved in the future, so committing stuff to writing for posterity without giving it any thought is a risky business. So, the idea of 'think before you write' is wise counsel.

96. Don't rely on common sense

So-called 'common sense' is often not common (different people have different ideas about what is common sense) and not always sense (it is often contradictory). What counts as common sense can be important advice and wisdom built up over many years of experience. However, it can also, at times, be based on unquestioned prejudices and taken-for-granted assumptions. But, whether what counts as common sense is sound or not, what resorting to common sense amounts to is relying on preformed ideas instead of using reflective practice to think, plan, analyse and make sense of the situations we are dealing with. Someone saying: 'It's common sense' is often inviting us to accept their perspective uncritically, rather than work out our own view on it.

97. Don't drop hints

Speaking openly and honestly is more likely to be effective than dropping hints. This is because: (i) people often don't tune in to the hint; it goes over their head; and (ii) if they do get it, they may resent it – they may feel that you are trying to manipulate them, rather than communicate with them in a genuine way. Despite these problems with hinting, it is a very common occurrence for people to risk alienating others in this way. Learning and practising the skills involved in sensitive and tactful direct communication without ruffling anyone's feathers are much wiser steps to take.

98. Take account of trauma

The term 'trauma' is often used in a very loose and 'watered down' way to refer to any difficult or distressing situation. However, in its technical sense, trauma refers to a wound (physical or psychological) that has lasting effects. We are now realizing more fully that so many of the mental health problems that people encounter are linked to earlier experiences of one or more traumas. Indeed, difficulties in life more broadly will often have their roots in trauma. So, if we are working with people in any sort of supportive or supervisory way, we would do well to ask ourselves whether trauma is playing any part in the situation – particularly those situations that are proving problematic or challenging in some way.

99. Smile!

Yes, it's a cliché, but the fact remains that, in working with people and their problems, we are likely to get better results if we smile. Smiling gives a clear message to the effect of 'I am pleased to be in your company' while not smiling can give the message that we are not pleased to be in that person's company. Of course, we don't want to go overboard and come across as insincere, but smiling really can make a big difference. Sounds obvious? Not worth saying? Just watch people around you and see how often people interact with one another without smiling. You'll see that lots of opportunities to make a positive connection are being missed.

100. Value your time

There are relatively few people in today's world of work who are not under time pressures. This is all the more reason that we need to make sure that our time is used wisely. This is not about petty ways of saving 30 seconds here or a minute and a half there, but rather about having the assertiveness skills to protect our valuable time by not allowing others to seduce us into putting time and effort into activities that are not a priority for us. Demands on our time are potentially infinite, but however skilful we are at time management, the time available will always be finite. Don't let it be spent too cheaply.

101. Bullying is not strong leadership

Many times I have heard some people try to justify bullying behaviours by describing oppressive practices as 'strong leadership'. In reality, using bullying tactics is a sign of a lack of leadership. A leader is someone who shapes a culture and creates an atmosphere where people want to do well, where they want to be part of a team that works well – they do not need to be coerced or intimidated into doing what is required of them. They feel they belong to an important endeavour and are pleased to be part of it. Bullying is a sign that leadership skills are lacking or that the person in a leadership role has failed to grasp what leadership is all about.

Conclusion

People are fascinating. As a species we can do enormous harm to one another and to our environment. But we can also do some extremely positive and worthwhile things. Which direction we go in, positive and constructive or negative and destructive, depends on a number of factors. But one of them is our own ability to influence situations in a positive direction. These tips – and the thoughts and learning they are intended to trigger – have been provided to help you play your part in trying to focus on the positives and safeguard against the negatives.

Of course, these tips will not be enough on their own, but it is my hope that they will play at least a small part in helping you move forward positively.

References

Archard, D. (2004) *Children: Rights and Childhood*, 2nd edn, London, Routledge.

Barry, B. (2005) *Why Social Justice Matters*, Cambridge, Polity.

Black, C. (2008) *Working for a Healthier Tomorrow*, London, The Stationery Office.

Boldt, L. G. (1999) *Zen and the Art of Making a Living: A Practical Guide to Creative Career Design*, London, Penguin.

Bolton, S. C. (ed.) (2007) *Dimensions of Dignity at Work*, London, Butterworth-Heinemann.

Boniwell, I. and Tunariu, A. D. (2019) *Positive Psychology: Theory, Research and Applications*, Maidenhead, Open University Press.

Briers, S. (2012) *Psychobabble: Exploding the Myths of the Self-help Generation*, Harlow, Pearson.

Castiglione, D., van Deth, J. W. and Wolleb, G. (eds) (2008) *The Handbook of Social Capital*, Oxford, Oxford University Press.

Corby, B. (2005) *Child Abuse: Towards a Knowledge Base*, 3rd edn, Maidenhead, Open University Press.

Covey, S. (1999) *The 7 Habits of Highly Effective People*, London, Simon & Schuster.

Coyte, M. E., Gilbert, P. and Nicholls, V. (eds) (2007) *Spirituality, Values and Mental Health: Jewels for the Journey*, London, Jessica Kingsley.

Dienstag, J. F. (2006) *Pessimism: Philosophy, Ethic, Spirit*, Princeton, NJ, Princeton University Press.

Haidt, J. (2006) *The Happiness Hypothesis*, London, Arrow Books.

Hedges, C. (2009) *Empire of Illusion: The End of Literacy and the Triumph of Spectacle*, New York, NY, Nation Books.

Hockey, J. and James, A. (1993) *Growing up and Growing Old*, London, Sage.

James, O. (2007) *Affluenza*, London, Vermilion.

James, O. (2008) *The Selfish Capitalist*, London, Vermilion.

Jordan, B. (2007) *Social Work and Well-being,* Lyme Regis, Russell House Publishing.

Kinder, A., Hughes, R. and Cooper, C. L. (eds) (2008) *Employee Wellbeing Support: A Workplace Resource*, Chichester, Wiley.

Layard, R. (2006) *Happiness: Lessons from a New Science*, London, Penguin.

Macdonald, L. A. C. (2005) *Wellness at Work: Protecting and Promoting Employee Wellbeing*, London, Chartered Institute of Personnel and Development.

McMahon, D. (2007) *The Pursuit of Happiness: A History from the Greeks to the Present*, London, Penguin.

Micklethwait, J. and Wooldridge, J. (1996) *The Witch Doctors: What the Management Gurus are Saying, Why it Matters and How to Make Sense of It*, London, Mandarin.

Moss, B. (2005) *Religion and Spirituality*, Lyme Regis, Russell House Publishing.

Percy-Smith, B. and Thomas, N. (eds) (2009) *A Handbook of Children and Young People's Participation: Perspectives from Theory and Practice*, London, Routledge.

Ricard, M. (2006) *Happiness: A Guide to Developing Life's Most Important Skill*, London, Atlantic Books.

Ricard, M. (2013) *Altruism: The Power of Compassion to Change Yourself and the World*, New York, Little, Brown.

Sartre, J-P. (2000) *Huis Clos and Other Plays*, London, Penguin.

Seligman, M. (2006) *Learned Optimism: How to Change Your Mind and Your Life*, London, Nicholas Brealey.

Thompson, N. (2015) *People Skills*, 4th edn, London, Palgrave.

Thompson, N. (2017) *Social Problems and Social Justice*, London, Palgrave.

Thompson, N. (2018) *Promoting Equality: Working with Diversity and Difference*, 4th edn, London, Palgrave.

Thompson, N. (2019) *The Managing Stress Practice Manual*, Wrexham, Avenue Media Solutions.

Thompson, N. and Bates, J. (eds) (2009) *Promoting Workplace Well-being*, Basingstoke, Palgrave Macmillan.

Thompson, N. and Moss, B. (2019) *Meaning, Values and Spirituality: A Learning and Development Manual*, 2nd edn, Hove, Pavilion.

Thompson, S. and Thompson, N. (2018) *The Critically Reflective Practitioner*, 2nd edn, London, Palgrave.

Wilkinson, R. and Pickett, K. (2010) *The Spirit Level: Why More Equal Societies Always Almost Do Better*, London, Allen Lane.

Wilkinson, R. and Pickett, K. (2018) *The Inner Level: How More Equal Societies Reduce Stress, Restore Sanity and Improve Everyone's Well-being*, London, Allen Lane,

Other learning resources by Neil Thompson

Neil has over 40 years' experience of helping people learn. He does this in a variety of ways, ranging from face-to-face training and conference presentations, through books, training manuals and articles to e-learning courses and online tuition.

Neil has over 40 books to his name and a growing number of e-books. He has also been involved in developing a number of training and development manuals and DVDs.

He has also been involved in developing a range of online learning materials, including e-learning courses and the *Avenue Professional Development Programme*, a subscription-based online learning community. It includes: discussion forums with tutor input from Neil; a growing library of multimedia learning resources; an e-portfolio and reflective journal; one e-book to help structure learning and another to review progress; and other facilities. Further information is available from **www.apdp.org.uk**.

E-courses

Dealing with Stress
Managing Stress (follow-up course specifically for managers)
Emotional Competence: Developing Emotional Intelligence and Resilience
Handling Aggression
Time and Workload Management
Learning to Learn
Getting Started with Reflective Practice
Equality, Diversity and Inclusion

Available from www.avenuemediasolutions.com/shop.

Books

People Management (Palgrave Macmillan, 2013)

People Skills (4th edn, Palgrave, 2015)

The Authentic Leader (Palgrave, 2016)

Promoting Equality (4th edn, Palgrave, 2018)

Effective Communication (3rd edn, Palgrave, 2018)

Applied Sociology (Routledge, 2018)

Mental Health and Well-being: Alternatives to the Medical Model (Routledge, 2019)

Information about all Neil's work can be found at **www.NeilThompson.info**.

Connect with Neil online

Neil has a strong online presence and welcomes connection. To find out more, visit **www.NeilThompson.info.**

Sign up for a free subscription to THE *humansolutions* BULLETIN e-zine. Subscribe now at **www.humansolutions.org.uk.** The Bulletin is part of the *humansolutions* website which provides information about a range of workplace and community problems and potential solutions

You can also subscribe for free to the *Learn with Neil Thompson* YouTube channel and you will then be able to see new videos as they are added. It is at: **https://bit.ly/2OoE6OR.**

Other Avenue Media Solutions Learning Resources

Practice manuals

Thompson, N. (2018) *The Social Worker's Practice Manual.*

Thompson, N. (2019) *The Learning from Practice Manual.*

Thompson, S. (2019) *The Care of Older People Practice Manual.*

Thompson, N. (2019) *The Managing Stress Practice Manual*

Other titles are in preparation.

E-books

Mann, H. (2013) *Sleep and Sleep Disorders: A Brief Introduction.*

Mann, H. (2016) *The Cancer Challenge: Coping with Cancer When Someone You Love is Diagnosed.*

Thompson, N. (2012) *Effective Teamwork: How to Develop a Successful Team.*

Thompson, N. (2013) *Effective Writing.*

Thompson, N. (2015) *How to do Social Work.*

Thompson, N. (2016) *A Career in Social Work.*

Thompson, S. and Wallace, R. (2015) *Tackling Low Self-esteem: Building Confidence and Self-respect.*

www.avenuemediasolutions.com

Printed in Poland
by Amazon Fulfillment
Poland Sp. z o.o., Wrocław